A GUIDE
TO THE GRADING OF
UNITED STATES COINS

A GUIDE
TO THE GRADING OF
UNITED STATES COINS
(ILLUSTRATED)

by

MARTIN R. BROWN

and

JOHN W. DUNN

WHITMAN PUBLISHING COMPANY

RACINE, WISCONSIN

1964

No. 9096

PUBLISHER'S PREFACE

A harmonious arrangement between Messrs. Brown and Dunn and the Whitman Publishing Co. has brought about a new, improved version of the well-known, standard reference book A GUIDE TO THE GRADING OF UNITED STATES COINS.

Brief grading descriptions following the Brown and Dunn standards have been spotted in the Whitman catalogs A GUIDE BOOK OF UNITED STATES COINS and HANDBOOK OF UNITED STATES COINS since 1962. Moreover valuations of the coins in those catalogs have been based on Brown and Dunn gradings.

Now you, the reader has in his hands a larger volume, because the addition of illustrations has approximately doubled the number of pages. Another improvement is the binding. Obviously the rounded back and sewed pages make for easy opening, and the board covers add lasting qualities so important in a constantly used reference book.

The line drawing illustrations represent the farthest advance in coin grading to date. Strictly speaking they are diagrams. Placed as they are, adjacent to each paragraph of word-description, the task of arriving at the condition of any coin becomes pleasantly accurate. The artist Arthur Mueller has done an outstanding job of reproducing each United States coin type. Important details are accurately located and the portraiture is surprisingly recognizable. The sizes of all diagrams are larger, in greater or lesser degree, than the true dimensions of the coins they represent. This permits a separation of details and somewhat approaches the scale one would encounter when a coin is viewed under a magnifying glass.

Authors Brown and Dunn have made some clarification changes in the text. No change in standards has been incorporated in such revisions.

The pages which follow contain the same introductory information contained in the original editions, as well as the appendix on cleaning coins. We feel certain that the reader will find this new guide to grading one of the most useful instruments to mature coin collecting yet devised.

Whitman Publishing Co.

INTRODUCTION

Shortly after the close of World War II, coin collecting began its phe-
nominal boom. How much of this can be attributed to a genuine interest
in the hobby and how much to speculation is a matter of argument.

The fact remains, however, that there are today thousands of new collectors. How much these newcomers to the field of numismatics know
about the grading of circulated United States coins is not known definitely.

The average collector depends to a great extent on the opinions of the
dealer from whom he buys. Reputable dealers, of course, exercise every
care in the grading of coins which they offer for sale. But collectors are
buying continually from many different sources.

Standardization of the grading of coins has been a slow process. Many
of the older dealers and collectors grade almost by instinct. They have
handled coins so much and examined so many in all kinds of conditions,
they automatically assign a grade to a coin. The "why" and the "how"
they do this is not reduced so easily to words. Then there are some who
feel that to reveal facts about the grading of coins is to give away trade
secrets.

The idea has prevailed among collectors and dealers that the grading
of coins is a matter of personal opinion and that no two people will grade
the same coin alike. This has been repeated so often that it has become
axiomatic.

Standards can be set up for the various grades of circulated United
States coins. Naturally, a person using these standards will have to make
decisions as to whether or not a coin meets certain standards.

The authors have had many years' experience in the field of numismatics.
They have surveyed carefully all types of United States coins and have
arrived at what can be considered fair and recognizable standards by
which circulated United States coins can be graded by collectors if reason-
able care is exercised.

However, the fact remains that the more experience the collector has
had and the more varied that experience has been with different kinds,
types and conditions of coins, the more confidence he will have in using
a standard grading system.

The authors recognize six principal categories in their grading system
of circulated United States coins: GOOD (G);VERY GOOD (VG); FINE
(F); VERY FINE (VF); EXTREMELY FINE(XF); ABOUT UNCIR-
CULATED (AU). In some of the earlier U. S. issues and for some of the

scarcer coins, there may be added two other grades; FAIR (FR) and ABOUT GOOD (ABT.G.).

Dealers will sometimes advertise coins that are graded G-VG, VG-F, F-VF, VF-XF. Or the description may be ABT. G. or VG plus, etc. This means that the coin in question more than meets minimum standards for the lower grade but is not quite good enough for the higher grade. To illustrate: A Liberty Head nickel to be GOOD need not show any of the LIBERTY on the crown but one graded VERY GOOD must have at least three letters of the word LIBERTY on the crown showing. Such a nickel with one or even two of the letters in LIBERTY showing could hardly be called GOOD or VERY GOOD; hence such a coin should be graded GOOD-VERY GOOD or GOOD plus.

Even in uncirculated coins there are grades. A coin may be strictly UNCIRCULATED and yet not exactly a perfect coin. This may be due to a poor job at the Mint or bad handling by the Mint and distribution agencies, causing rim nicks, scratches, scuffed places. Larger coins — dollars, half dollars and even quarter dollars — because of their weight tend to be scratched and nicked as they are handled and shipped in bags.

For UNCIRCULATED coins, the more choice specimens — free from rim nicks, scratches, scuffed places and perfectly struck — are more desirable. They are described by various trade names: Choice, A-1, Select, Gem.

The collector who desires to grade a circulated U. S. coin should develop a routine. If he is not familiar with the type of coin he is grading, he should make every effort to examine an UNCIRCULATED specimen under a good magnifying glass. A substitute for this procedure is a picture of an UNCIRCULATED specimen. By doing so, he can become familiar with the design of the coin.

In examining a coin to be graded, the collector should notice carefully the general condition of the coin. He should observe if the piece has ever been in a fire, giving the metal a hard black or brown surface; if the coin is corroded badly, has ever been exposed to acid or mercury; if there are any bad scratches, gouges, rim nicks or poorly struck letters or numerals. Of course, he must remember that such things as file marks on the rims of early U. S. coins and chop marks on Trade Dollars, for instance, are to be considered almost an integral part of the coin.

Coins which are badly worn or which have serious defects are not worth keeping unless the coin is an especially rare one. Where less serious defects exist — light rim nicks or scratches — the coin must be graded down at least one grade from whatever it might otherwise have been graded.

These preliminary steps are important and can be accomplished usually without the aid of a glass. More careful examination of the coin should be made with a good glass. This should be done under a good light and the coin should be looked at from various angles. This is important for often the condition of key points of a coin will not show up plainly from one angle but will be revealed if looked at from another point of view.

In examining the coin, the collector will keep in mind the requirements for the various grades for that particular denomination and type of coin. In doing so, the field will be narrowed to perhaps two grades. Closer and more careful inspection will usually enable the collector to grade the coin correctly. The average collector will have very little trouble with the grades GOOD, VERY GOOD and FINE. For VERY FINE, EX-TREMELY FINE and ABOUT UNCIRCULATED grades, even more careful and detailed study may be required.

Beginning collectors have a tendency to overgrade a coin. It is always better to undergrade a coin, about which there is any doubt, than to overgrade.

No attempt has been made to "dress up" the terminology used in describing the requirements for the various grades. The language used is that of the coin shop and collector of experience. The collector who uses this book will soon become familiar with the descriptive words and phrases which should become a part of the collector's coin vocabulary.

All the details which may be considered in examining and grading a coin have not been covered. The collector will find that certain key points in the design of a coin have been selected and very specifically pointed out in order to simplify procedures. If these points meet certain standards, then the rest of the coin will usually follow suit. Also the collector will note that descriptions of conditions for the various grades are considered by the accepted types of United States coins rather than a multiplicity of varieties within a type.

The authors have not included in this edition American colonial coins, private issues of gold or U. S. silver and gold commemoratives.

Valuations of coins are not given. That is not the purpose of this book. The collector will find reliable information which will serve as a guide in determining various conditions in circulated U. S. coins and in recognizing fakes of certain well known coins that are frequently offered for sale.

MARTIN R. BROWN, ANA 5508

JOHN W. DUNN, ANA 25,156

January, 1958

This edition of A GUIDE TO THE GRADING OF UNITED STATES COINS represents the second major revision of the book since its first appearance in 1958. We believe this edition represents the ultimate, combining a number of features which will make the book more valuable to the beginning as well as the advanced collector of United States coins. Not the least of these are the pictorial representations of the various grades for the different types and denominations of U. S. coins.

Basically, the B & D GRADING SYSTEM which has come to be accepted by thousands of collectors and dealers as the standard or point of reference for grading United States coins remains the same with a few very important revisions and corrections. Please be assured the authors are constantly alert to consider those changes which will make A GUIDE TO THE GRADING OF UNITED STATES COINS the very finest book of its kind in the world.

Again, we would like to emphasize that not all of the details which may be considered in examining and grading a coin have been covered. The B & D System is a "working system" for collectors to remember and use easily. The collector will find that certain KEY points in the design of a coin have been selected and specifically pointed out visually and verbally in order to simplify procedures. If these points meet certain standards, then the rest of the coin will usually follow suit.

This book does not seek to give any valuations of coins. For the standard reference on retail valuations, see the latest edition of and supplements to A GUIDE BOOK OF U. S. COINS by R. S. Yeoman.

M.R.B.

J.W.D.

January, 1964

CONTENTS

CONTENTS—*Continued*

**PLEASE READ THF INTRODUCTION CAREFULLY. MUCH VALU-
ABLE INFORMATION IS CONTAINED IN THE NEXT FOUR PAGES**

1793

There are two distinct types of obverses for this period. For the 1793 Half Cent, the bust of Liberty with flowing hair faces left. A Liberty Cap is on a pole over her right shoulder. **LIBERTY** in circular arrangement is above the head and the date is underneath the bust.

For the reverse, a wreath of two olive branches tied at the bottom with a ribbon in a bow knot encloses the denomination, **HALF CENT**; below the knot of ribbon is the fraction 1/200; above and around the wreath is the legend, **UNITED STATES OF AMERICA**.

1794-1797

For the obverse, the bust of Liberty with flowing hair faces right. A Liberty Cap is over her left shoulder, with and without a pole. **LIBERTY** in circular arrangement is above the head and the date is underneath the bust.

For the reverse, the design is the same as for the 1793 Half Cent.

Coins of this period were struck from horse-drawn presses. They should be graded from the obverse rather than the reverse side. Very few coins of these years will be well struck on both sides. The few Half Cents of this period that are well struck on both sides are very scarce and should command a higher market value.

HALF CENTS

FAIR

Coin will be identified as to date and type.

ABOUT GOOD

Date will be fairly plain. Rest of the coin will be very much worn.

GOOD

Bust of Liberty and the Liberty Cap will be outlined but show no details. Date will be plain.

VERY GOOD

Liberty's hair will show some details.

FINE

About two-thirds of Liberty's hair from top of head to bottom of neck will be worn but will show some detail.

VERY FINE

Hair above Liberty's ear and forehead will be worn with some detail. Balance of hair will be detailed and distinct.

HALF CENTS

EXTREMELY FINE

Hair above ear and forehead will be well detailed but will show definite wear.

ABOUT UNCIRCULATED

There will be a trace of wear only on Liberty's hair above her forehead and on the highest point of her shoulder.

HALF CENT—Draped Bust, 1800-1808

For the obverse, the draped bust of Liberty faces right. Her hair is fastened by a narrow fillet or band ending behind the head in a knot with flowing ends. Her hair falls downward over her shoulders and terminates in small ringlets. Above the head is **LIBERTY** and below the bust is the date. The reverse is the same as for the Liberty Cap Type of 1793-1797.

FAIR

Coin will be identified as to date and type.

ABOUT GOOD

Rim will be worn down into lettering on reverse. Date will be readable but not perfect.

HALF CENTS

GOOD

Liberty's bust will be outlined but show no detail. All lettering and the date must be plain but will be worn.

VERY GOOD

Major detail of drapery on front of Liberty's bust will show and continue about half way around to Liberty's shoulder. Date and lettering must be plain.

FINE

Hair above forehead and to the left of Liberty's eye will be worn smooth but all other hair detail will be well defined. Shoulder will be worn but all other detail of drapery on bust will show.

VERY FINE

Hair above Liberty's forehead and to the left of her eye will be outlined and show considerable detail. Leaves of olive branches on reverse will show only slight wear.

EXTREMELY FINE

Hair above forehead and to the left of Liberty's eye will be well outlined and detailed. Leaves of olive branches on reverse will be well outlined and show only slight wear.

HALF CENTS

ABOUT UNCIRCULATED

There will be a trace of wear on highest points of the obverse and reverse, including hair above forehead, shoulder and bust; leaves of olive branches, bow and knot of ribbon on reverse.

HALF CENT — Turban Head, 1809-1836

For the obverse, the heavy-featured head of Liberty faces left. A band on which is inscribed **LIBERTY** in small letters confines her hair. The hair falls in short curls over her forehead and temple and in longer curls over her shoulder. There is actually no turban, but the band of ribbon and hair arrangement combine to give that effect. Stars are on either side of head.

For the reverse, a wreath of laurel, formed of a single branch and with leaves in clusters, encloses the words, **HALF CENT**. The ends of the wreath are tied together with a short broad ribbon. **UNITED STATES OF AMERICA** is in circular arrangement around the wreath.

FAIR

Coin will be identified as to date and type.

ABOUT GOOD

Rim will be worn down into stars on obverse and lettering on reverse.

HALF CENTS

GOOD

A partial **LIBERTY** will show on Liberty's headband. Date, stars and letters in legends will be plain although worn.

VERY GOOD

Complete **LIBERTY** will show on the headband. The ear will be visible. Hair curl below the ear and center of neck will be outlined plainly but will be worn smooth. All letters in legends must be plain. There must be a fairly good rim for both obverse and reverse.

FINE

Letters "I" and "B" in **LIBERTY** will be rather weak. Hair below "I" and "B" in **LIBERTY** will be outlined but worn. Hair above "R" and "T" will be outlined but worn.

VERY FINE

LIBERTY will be strong. Edges of headband will be sharp. Hair above "R" and "T" and below "I" and "B" in **LIBERTY** will be well defined but show definite wear.

EXTREMELY FINE

Hair will be sharp but there will be wear on rounded detail.

HALF CENTS

ABOUT UNCIRCULATED

Only a trace of wear will show on the highest points, including hair above "R" and "T" and below "I" and "B" of **LIBERTY**. Only a trace of wear will show on leaves of wreath and knot of ribbon on reverse.

HALF CENT — Braided Hair, 1840-1857

For the obverse, a classic type of Liberty head faces left. Hair just above the eyes is braided. Above is a coronet on which is inscribed **LIB-ERTY**. Hair is combed straight back from coronet to form a series of knots each of which is bound with a beaded hair cord. Hair falls in grace-ful curls to a point below the bust. Thirteen stars in circular arrangement around the head and the date is underneath the bust.

For the reverse, a wreath of laurel encloses the words, **HALF CENT**. The wreath stems are tied at bottom with ribbon in a bow knot. **UNITED STATES OF AMERICA** is in circular arrangement around wreath.

FAIR

Coin will be identified as to type and date.

ABOUT GOOD

There will be no **LIBERTY** on the headband. The reverse will be readable but very much worn.

[19]

HALF CENTS

GOOD

There will be a partial **LIBERTY** on the headband and some of the beads on the hair cords will show.

VERY GOOD

The beads on the hair cords will be distinct but rather worn. There will be only a few details for Liberty's hair. Full **LIBERTY** but worn.

FINE

Horizontal hairlines to the right of Liberty's ear will be worn flat. Curls on the lower part of the neck will be outlined but show few details. Beads on hair cords around hair knots must be very distinct.

VERY FINE

Curls on lower part of Liberty's neck will be detailed except that the very bottom curl will show only a few details.

EXTREMELY FINE

Bottom curl on Liberty's neck will be well detailed with only the highest parts showing slight wear.

ABOUT UNCIRCULATED

There will be a trace of wear on Liberty's hair right of ear and hair curls on lower part of neck and below bust. Only a trace of wear will show on leaves of laurel wreath and bow on reverse.

LARGE CENT — Chain Reverse, 1793

For the obverse, the head of Liberty faces right. The hair is disshevelled as though facing a strong wind. The bust is short ending in a point; above the head is the word **LIBERTY**; below the bust, the date.

For the reverse, the denomination, **ONE CENT**, and the fraction, 1/100, are enclosed by an endless chain of thirteen links. The whole is encircled by the legend, **UNITED STATES OF AMERICA** or **UNITED STATES OF AMERI**.

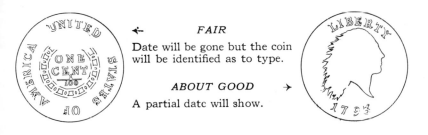

←   *FAIR*

Date will be gone but the coin will be identified as to type.

ABOUT GOOD   →

A partial date will show.

GOOD

The denomination, **ONE CENT**, must show in the center of the chain. Lettering around the edge on reverse will be worn but readable. Date must show.

LARGE CENTS

VERY GOOD

Date must be complete. On the reverse, all of the lettering must be plain and readable.

FINE

Links of the chain will be worn but must be complete. Hair will be well outlined but will be worn smooth from top of head to bottom of neck.

VERY FINE

Ear of Liberty must show. Hair above the ear, although worn, will be farily well detailed.

EXTREMELY FINE

Highest points of the hair, including that back of Liberty's temple, will show definite wear.

ABOUT UNCIRCULATED

There will be a trace of wear on the highest portions of the hair from the jaw line to top of Liberty's head.

Special Notation: There are many imperfections in this series, including weak strikes, letters not struck up, etc.

LARGE CENT — Single Bow Wreath, 1793

For the obverse, head of Liberty faces right with her hair falling in heavy separated masses, terminating in pointed locks. Above the head, LIBERTY. Below the bust is date and between bust and date is a sprig of three leaves on some varieties.

For the reverse, there is a wreath formed of two curving branches of laurel with sprays of berries and trefoils. The wreath is tied at the bottom with a ribbon. Within the wreath is ONE CENT. Below the bow of ribbon is the fraction, 1/100. Around the wreath is the legend, UNITED STATES OF AMERICA.

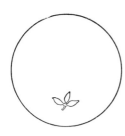

FAIR

Coin will be identified as of this type by the sprig of olive above the date. Date will be practically gone.

← **ABOUT GOOD**

Portion of the date must be readable.

GOOD →

Date will be readable but worn.

LARGE CENTS

VERY GOOD

All lettering and date on obverse must show. On reverse, all of the berries in the wreath must show even though they are worn. Letters on reverse must be distinct.

FINE

At least two-thirds of Liberty's hair will be worn away but some of the hair detail will show.

VERY FINE

Approximately one-half of Liberty's hair from ear to crown of her head will be worn but will show considerable detail. The ear must show.

EXTREMELY FINE

Only a portion of the hair above the ear will show considerable wear. There will be slight wear on Liberty's hair from the ear to the bottom of the bust.

ABOUT UNCIRCULATED

There will be a trace of wear on the highest portions of the hair just back of the temple and on the highest portions of the reverse.

LARGE CENT — Liberty Cap, 1793-1796

For the obverse, the head of Liberty faces right. Her hair falls in heavy separated strands behind her shoulder; short curly strands are brushed back from her temple. Liberty Cap is on a pole over her left shoulder.

For the reverse, a wreath of two olive branches tied with a ribbon encloses ONE CENT. Between the long ends of the ribbon is the fraction, 1/100. The wreath is encircled almost by UNITED STATES OF AMERICA. The edge bears inscription, ONE HUNDRED FOR A DOLLAR.

FAIR

Coin will be identified as to date and type.

ABOUT GOOD

Date will be fairly plain. Rest of the coin will be worn.

LARGE CENTS

GOOD

Bust of Liberty and the Liberty Cap will be outlined but show no detail. Date will be plain. Letters on reverse will be worn in spots.

VERY GOOD

All lettering on reverse will show.

FINE

About two-thirds of Liberty's hair from top of head to bottom of neck will be worn but will show some detail.

VERY FINE

Hair above Liberty's ear and forehead will be worn with some detail. Balance of hair will be detailed and distinct.

EXTREMELY FINE

Hair above ear and forehead of Liberty will be well defined but will show definite wear.

LARGE CENTS

ABOUT UNCIRCULATED

There will be only slight wear on Liberty's hair above her forehead and on the highest point of her shoulder.

Special Notation: The 1793 issues are usually weaker struck than 1794.

LARGE CENT — Draped Bust, 1796-1807

For the obverse, a draped bust of Liberty faces right. Her hair is fastened by a narrow band ending behind the head in a knot of ribbon. Her hair then flows downward over her shoulders and terminates in small ringlets. Above the head is **LIBERTY** in large letters. Below the bust is the date. The reverse is the same as for the Liberty Cap Type.

FAIR

Coin will be identified as to date and type.

ABOUT GOOD

Rim will be worn down into lettering on reverse. Date will be readable but not perfect.

LARGE CENTS

GOOD

Bust of Liberty will be outlined but show no detail. All lettering and date must be plain but will be worn. On some dates, the denomination — **ONE CENT** — will be weak.

←   *VERY GOOD*

Major detail of drapery on front of Liberty's bust will show faintly. Date and lettering must be plain.

FINE   →

Hair above Liberty's forehead and to the left of her eye will be worn smooth but all other hair detail will be well defined. Shoulder will be worn but all details of drapery on bust will show.

VERY FINE

Hair above Liberty's forehead and to the left of her eye will be outlined and show large amount of detail. Leaves of the olive branches on reverse will show only slight amount of wear.

EXTREMELY FINE

Hair above forehead and to the left of Liberty's eye will be well detailed. Leaves of olive branches on reverse will be outlined well and show some wear only on highest portions.

[28]

LARGE CENTS

ABOUT UNCIRCULATED

There will be a trace of wear only on the highest points, including hair above forehead, shoulder and bust on obverse; leaves of olive branches, bow and knot of ribbon on reverse.

Special Notation: It is characteristic of coins of this denomination and type to have small portions of the planchet clipped, the denomination ONE CENT struck weakly, planchet blisters, and various portions of the coin struck weakly. In some instances, one side — either obverse or reverse — will be struck lighter than the other.

LARGE CENT — Turban Head, 1808-1814

For the obverse, the head of Liberty faces left. The bust is broad and cut nearly square in front. A band on which is inscribed LIBERTY in small letters confines the hair which falls in short curls over the forehead and temple. Longer curls hang over the shoulder. There is actually no turban but the band of ribbon and the hair arrangement give that effect. There are seven stars in circular arrangement to the left of the head and six stars to the right. Date is underneath the bust.

For the reverse, a wreath of laurel, formed of a single branch with leaves in clusters, encloses the word, ONE CENT. Wreath ends are tied at bottom with a bow of ribbon which is short and broad. A bar is under the word, CENT. UNITED STATES OF AMERICA is around wreath. Edge is plain.

FAIR

Coin will be identified as to date and type.

LARGE CENTS

ABOUT GOOD

Rim will be worn into top of letters on reverse.

GOOD

Date, stars and letters in legends must be plain although worn.

VERY GOOD

LIBERTY on headband must be plain. Ear must be visible. Hair above eye will be worn smooth. Curl below ear and in the middle of neck will be outlined plainly although worn. All lettering on reverse must be plain. There will be a fairly good rim for both obverse and reverse.

FINE

Ear will be sharp. Hair below ear to tip of curl must be fairly well defined. Hair above Liberty's eye will be outlined but worn almost smooth as well as hair in front of ear.

LARGE CENTS

VERY FINE

Hair in front of and below Liberty's ear must be very plain but will show definite wear. Hair above eye will be outlined with some detail. Eyebrow will be well developed. High points of leaves or reverse will show wear.

EXTREMELY FINE

Hair in front of and below ear must be sharp with very slight wear on high points. Hair above eye will be well defined but show some wear.

ABOUT UNCIRCULATED

There will be a trace of wear above Liberty's eye and below the "L" in LIBERTY. Leaves of wreath and the ribbon on reverse will show only slight wear.

LARGE CENT — Coronet, 1816-1839

For obverse, a heavy featured head of Liberty faces left. Hair is combed back from coronet and ends in two knots each of which is tied into shape with a beaded hair cord. Stray locks project out from beneath coronet.

LARGE CENTS

Portion of her hair falls in curls below bust. Around head are thirteen six-pointed stars and date is underneath bust.

For the reverse, a wreath of laurel encloses words, **ONE CENT**. Ends of wreath are tied with ribbon in bow knot. **UNITED STATES OF AMERICA** encircles wreath.

FAIR

Coin will be identified as to type and date.

ABOUT GOOD

Rim will be worn down into top of letters on reverse. Date will be readable.

GOOD

All letters in legends and date must stand out with even wear. Head of Liberty will show little or no detail.

VERY GOOD

LIBERTY on headband must be plain. The date, stars and all letters in legends must be plain. Major details of hair must show. About one-half of the back hair cord must show.

LARGE CENTS

FINE

Both hair cords around knots of hair must be complete although they will show weakly. There will be considerable detail in hair lines.

VERY FINE

Both hair cords must stand out although they will be worn. Wavy strand of hair along inside hair cord must be well defined. Considerable detail must be present for hair above coronet and around ear.

EXTREMELY FINE

Both hair cords must stand out sharply. Wavy strand of hair which follows inner hair cord must be fairly sharp.

ABOUT UNCIRCULATED

Only slight wear will show on all high spots of coin, including hair just above the eye on obverse and leaves in wreath and ribbon on reverse.

Special Notation: Some of the cents of 1836 and 1839 are not struck boldly on obverse. This is especially true of the date of the 1836 coin.

LARGE CENT — Braided Hair, 1840-1857

For the obverse, a more classic head of Liberty faces left. Hair just above the eye is braided. Above is a coronet on which is inscribed LIBERTY. Hair is combed straight back from coronet to form series of two knots each of which is bound with a hair cord. Hair falls in graceful curls around head. Thirteen stars are around head; date is underneath bust.

For the reverse, a wreath of laurel encloses words, **ONE CENT**. Wreath stems are tied at the bottom with ribbon in bow knot. **UNITED STATES OF AMERICA** encircles the wreath.

FAIR

Not collectable.

ABOUT GOOD

Lettering and date will be weak.

GOOD

Both obverse and reverse will be worn greatly. However, all of the word **LIBERTY** on the headband must show although the top of the letters will be worn considerably.

LARGE CENTS

VERY GOOD

Hair lines on top of Liberty's head and back of coronet will be worn smooth. All other hair lines on head below the ear will be worn but plain. Liberty's ear must be outlined.

FINE

Most of hair lines on top of Liberty's head and back of coronet will show but be worn. Hair braid above the eye will show. Ear will be well defined.

VERY FINE

Top two hair lines on top of Liberty's head and back of coronet will be worn together. Hair above the ear will be well defined but worn. Hair above the eye will be well defined but show wear.

EXTREMELY FINE

The top two hair lines on top of Liberty's head and back of the coronet will be worn in spots, especially towards the back. Hair above the ear will be detailed but worn slightly. Hair above the eyes will be sharp.

ABOUT UNCIRCULATED

There will be a trace of wear above the eye and above the ear. On reverse, there will be slight wear on leaves of laurel wreath and the bow of ribbon.

For the obverse, there is an eagle in full flight to the left. Date is at the bottom underneath the eagle. Legend, UNITED STATES OF AMERICA, is at the top in circular arrangement.

For the reverse, a wreath of corn, wheat, cotton and tobacco encloses the denomination, ONE CENT.

FAIR

Coin will be identified as to date and type. Date will be barely visible.

ABOUT GOOD

Date will be weak. Rim will be worn down into lettering on obverse.

GOOD

Coin will be worn very much but date and all lettering in legend and denomination must stand out.

VERY GOOD

The eye of the eagle must show. Outline of ends of feathers in right wing must show although some will be worn almost smooth.

SMALL CENTS

FINE

The eye and head of the eagle must be sharp. Outline of ends of feathers in the right wing of eagle will show with no ends missing or badly worn.

VERY FINE

The head and eye of the eagle will be very bold. Feathers in right wing and tail must show considerable detail. Outline of ends of feathers in right wing and tail must be plain with no ends missing or worn smooth.

EXTREMELY FINE

All feathers in both wings and tail of the eagle must be very plain. All feathers in breast of eagle will be plain but show some wear.

ABOUT UNCIRCULATED

Only a trace of wear will show on all high points: breast, head, thigh and wing tips of the eagle.

Special Notations: A small percentage of these coins were poorly struck, especially the 1857. Some 1857 Flying Eagle Cents show very poor date and lettering on obverse.

Grading of the 1856 Flying Eagle Cents (really patterns) follows the same procedure as for other dates of this series. It should be pointed out that most of the coins which were struck in 1856 were in **PROOF** and in several kinds of metal.

SMALL CENTS

The important thing about 1856 Flying Eagle Cents is to be able to recognize those that are genuine. Many fake 1856 Flying Eagle Cents are being offered for sale. All genuine cents of this date are of the Large Letter variety. Sometimes an 1857 cent is altered with the "7" being changed into a "6." These are quite apparent usually and are easily recognized upon close investigation.

Frequently an 1858 cent is used with the "8" being made into a "6." Often these jobs are quite crude and easily recognized. Then again the altered date is perfect even under a strong glass.

A sure test to determine the genuineness of an 1856 Flying Eagle Cent (where it is suspected an 1858 cent may have been altered) is as follows: draw an imaginary line down the stem of the figure "5" and continue this line down past the bottom of the date; if the 1856 cent is genuine, this imaginary line will cut off a portion of the curl of the figure "5"; if the cent has been changed from 1858 to 1856, the line will be tangent to the curl of the figure "5."

SMALL CENT — Indian Head, 1859-1909

For the obverse, an Indian girl's head is adorned with war bonnet on which is the word **LIBERTY** in raised letters. Ribbon on which **LIBERTY** appears continues down past hair curls and shows diamond designs. **UNITED STATES OF AMERICA** in circular arrangement above head.

For the 1859 reverse, a wreath of laurel encloses the denomination, **ONE CENT**. For the 1860-1909 reverse, a wreath of oak leaves with small heraldic shield at top between the ends of the wreath encloses the denomination, **ONE CENT**. The "S" mint mark for 1908 and 1909 issues is found on the reverse under ribbon of wreath. From 1859-1864, copper-nickel is used; from 1864-1909, bronze.

FAIR

Not collectable.

SMALL CENTS

ABOUT GOOD

Lettering will be partially worn away. Date will be visible.

GOOD

Indian girl's head will be well outlined with all feathers present but showing considerable wear. **LIBERTY** on headband will be worn smooth. Date and all letters in legends will be readable.

VERY GOOD

Any three letters of the word **LIBERTY** on the headband will show although the bottom of the letters may be weak.

FINE

Full LIBERTY on headband must be present with some of the letters worn but plain and readable.

VERY FINE

Full LIBERTY will show on headband with all letters sharp and showing even wear. Some of the diamond designs will show on the ribbon along the neck of the Indian girl. Letters "IBER" in LIBERTY must not be weak.

EXTREMELY FINE

LIBERTY on the headband will be strong with no letters worn. The feathers will be well defined with details sharp. There will be some wear above ear and curl to the right of the ribbon. Most of the diamond designs on ribbon will show plainly.

ABOUT UNCIRCULATED

Only a trace of wear will show on all high points, including hair above ear and hair curl to the right of ribbon. Only a very small amount of wear will show on the end of the ribbon.

Special Notation: For all 1864 "L" cents, the letter "L" must be readable, even for those in *GOOD* condition. Coins graded *ABOUT GOOD* of this date and with "L" will show a poor letter but must be good enough to be verified. On many *UNCIRCULATED* dates, the diamond designs will show up very poorly; hence on lesser grades, the diamond designs may show weakly if at all.

SMALL CENT — Lincoln, 1909 to Date

For the obverse, a bust of Abraham Lincoln, designed by Victor D. Brenner, faces right. IN GOD WE TRUST is at top above head; LIBERTY in small letters is in field of bust; date is at right of bust and mint mark (if any) is immediately underneath the date.

For the reverse, 1909-1958, an open wreath of stylized wheat stalks encloses the denomination, ONE CENT and the legend, UNITED STATES OF AMERICA. Motto, E PLURIBUS UNUM, is in circular arrangement at the top. For the first year of issue and only for a brief time, the designer's initials, VDB, appear in very small letters at the bottom of the reverse side and near the rim. Beginning with the year 1959, the reverse was changed to show the Lincoln Memorial in the center; immediately above in two straight lines is the motto, E PLURIBUS UNUM. At the top in circular arrangement, UNITED STATES OF AMERICA; at bottom in larger letters, ONE CENT.

The following grading is based on the 1909-1958 issues.

FAIR

Coin will be identified as to date and type.

ABOUT GOOD

Rim will be worn down into the top of letter of mottoes on obverse and reverse. Date and mint mark (if any) must be readable.

SMALL CENTS

GOOD

Wheat stalks on reverse will be worn smooth with no trace of the parallel lines in the upper part of wheat stalks. Date, mint mark (if any) and letters in legends and mottoes must be readable.

VERY GOOD

Wheat stalks should show some heads of grain. On one or both sides there should be at least one-half of the parallel lines in the upper part of the wheat stalk or stalks.

FINE

Parallel lines in upper part of the wheat stalks should show plainly and be separated even though they will be worn. The left or right wheat stalk may show some lines worn smooth at top and down the outer edge. Lincoln's ear and bow tie must be visible on obverse.

VERY FINE

All lines in right and left wheat stalks must be plain and sharp with no worn spots. Lincoln's ear on obverse must be well defined with some wear at the top of the ear. Bow tie lines must be very plain. Cheek and jawbones will be worn but clearly separated.

SMALL CENTS

EXTREMELY FINE

Parallel lines in each wheat stalk must be bold and clearly defined with no lines worn smooth. On obverse, lines of ear must be raised and sharp, especially at the top of the ear. Cheek and jawbones will be clearly defined although worn.

ABOUT UNCIRCULATED

Parallel lines in each wheat stalk must be very bold and clearly defined with only a trace of wear. On obverse, cheek and jawbone will show only a trace of wear on the very highest points.

Special Notation: Many coins of the issues of 1921, 1922, 1923 and 1924 were poorly struck. The obverse may be well struck with a poorly struck reverse or vice versa. After being in circulation, this condition becomes more noticeable. Due consideration must be taken in grading coins of these dates, the usual standards being relaxed somewhat. Many 1924-D cents have a weak mint mark and a tendency to be more boldly struck on one side than the other. Also a number of 1924-D cents in all grades will show on the reverse a depressed line, extending from the rim at top through the word **CENT**. It is not a diebreak and was not done outside of the mint.

1914-D cents, because of their rarity, are in great demand. Fake 1914-D cents are often offered for sale. Some 1914-D cents are made from 1944-D cents. These are easily recognized because the space between the "9" and the second "1" is too great.

Fake 1914-D cents are also made from 1914 cents. A "D" is stamped in the field of the coin below the 1914. Then the metal is cut away carefully from around the "D" leaving the "D" on a little mound. Close inspection with a good glass and holding the coin on a level with the eye will show that the top of the "D" is even with the surface of the remaining field and below the 1914.

Still another and more crude method is to solder a "D" onto the coin below a 1914 date. Again, close inspection will show clearly that the coin has had a "D" soldered onto the surface of the field.

Fake 1931-S cents are becoming more common. These are usually made from 1936-S cents, the "6" being changed into a "1." A strong glass will show easily that the fake "1" is extremely short.

SMALL CENTS

Fake 1943 "bronze cents" are made from regular bronze cents of 1948. Compare such suspected fakes with a genuine 1943 steel cent. A straight line drawn immediately underneath the date of a genuine 1943 cent will cut through the curl of the figure "3" at the bottom. On a fake cent, the bottom curl will be above the line.

LINCOLN MEMORIAL TYPE CENT

The following grading is based exclusively on the 1959 to date issues.

FINE

Lincoln's ear and bow tie must be visible on the obverse.

VERY FINE

Lincoln's ear on the obverse must be well defined with some wear at the top of the ear. Bow tie lines must be very plain. Cheek and jawbones will be worn but separated clearly.

EXTREMELY FINE

On obverse, lines of ear must be raised and sharp, especially at the top of the ear. Cheek and jaw lines will be defined clearly although worn.

ABOUT UNCIRCULATED

On obverse, cheek and jawbone will show only a trace of wear on the very highest points.

Special Notation: Grading for issues 1959 to date is based exclusively on the obverse.

See pictures of other issues of cent.

SMALL CENTS

TWO CENTS — Large and Small Motto, 1864-1875

For the obverse, the main device is a large shield in heraldic design. Two arrows are hidden by shield with only the heads and butts visible. An olive branch hangs on either side of the shield. At the top of the coin and above the shield is a broad ribbon with bold fold in center. On this ribbon is the motto, **IN GOD WE TRUST**.

For the reverse, a wreath of wheat with stems tied at the bottom by ribbon encloses the denomination, **TWO CENTS**. Around the wreath is the legend, **UNITED STATES OF AMERICA**.

FAIR

Coin will be identified as to denomination and date.

ABOUT GOOD

Motto will be worn away. All other lettering will be plain.

GOOD

IN GOD in motto must show plainly on obverse.

TWO CENTS

←   *VERY GOOD*

WE in motto must show even though weakly and not completely.

FINE   →

Complete motto, IN GOD WE TRUST, must show. The WE will be weak but plain.

←   *VERY FINE*

Entire motto, including WE, must be very plain.

EXTREMELY FINE   →

WE in motto, IN GOD WE TRUST, must stand out very boldly.

←   *ABOUT UNCIRCULATED*

There should be a trace of wear only on the WE in the motto on the obverse.

Special Notation: Small motto 1864 Two-cent pieces are not to be found in FAIR or ABOUT GOOD condition.

THREE CENTS — Nickel, 1865-1889

For the obverse, a classic head of Liberty faces left. There is an elaborate hair arrangement with flowing curls down the neck. Coronet is inscribed with word, **LIBERTY**. Date is at the bottom underneath the bust and **UNITED STATES OF AMERICA** in circular arrangement at top. For the reverse, a wreath of olive branches encloses a Roman numeral III.

FAIR

Not collectable.

ABOUT GOOD

Coin will be identified as a nickel Three-Cent piece with the date readable.

GOOD

Roman numeral III on reverse will be worn smooth. However, date and all letters in legends must be plain and readable.

VERY GOOD

At least one-half of the vertical lines within the Roman numeral III must show. There must be a complete rim for both the obverse and reverse.

THREE CENTS — Nickel

FINE

Hair curls of Liberty on obverse must be well outlined and show some detail.

VERY FINE

About half of Liberty's hair curls will show very plainly.

EXTREMELY FINE

Coin will show practically no wear but there will be no mint luster.

ABOUT UNCIRCULATED

Coin will show a faint trace of wear with some mint luster present.

Special Notation: Many nickel Three-Cent pieces were poorly struck with a weak **LIBERTY** on the headband on the obverse. In many cases, there are broken lines and even smooth spots in the Roman numeral III on the reverse, even in uncirculated specimens.

NICKEL FIVE CENTS — Shield, 1866-1883

For the obverse, there is a heraldic shield with a small formee cross on top as the main device. Within the shield, small horizontal raised lines fill the chief section; the base field contains six vertical columns made up of closely spaced raised lines. Two arrows are hidden with only the points and butts visible. An olive branch hangs on either side of shield. IN GOD WE TRUST in circular arrangement at the top and date underneath the shield.

For the reverse, 1866-1867, thirteen six-pointed stars alternating with rays encircle the numeral "5." UNITED STATES OF AMERICA at top; CENTS is at the bottom. For the reverse of 1867-1883, the rays are omitted. Otherwise the design is the same.

FAIR

Coin will be identified as a Shield nickel five-cent piece with the date barely visible.

ABOUT GOOD

IN GOD WE TRUST on obverse will be worn away but all other details will be plain.

GOOD

IN GOD WE TRUST and all letters in legends must be readable. The date must show plainly.

NICKEL FIVE CENTS

VERY GOOD

A fairly good rim must show for both the obverse and reverse. **IN GOD WE TRUST** must stand out very plainly. Some lines at the top of the shield must show.

FINE

Individual leaves of the olive branches on either side of the shield will be well outlined but from the tip to about halfway up individual leaves will be worn smooth.

VERY FINE

Individual leaves of the olive branches on either side of the shield will be well defined but the center line in the leaves will be worn away.

NICKEL FIVE CENTS

EXTREMELY FINE

Only the very tip of the leaves in the olive branches will show some wear. The cross atop the shield will show only slight wear on the outside lines.

ABOUT UNCIRCULATED

Only a faint trace of wear will show on the cross, shield and olive branches on the obverse and the numeral "5" on the reverse.

Special Notation: On many uncirculated coins of this issue, some lines in the top section of the shield may be faint.

NICKEL FIVE CENTS — Liberty Head, 1883-1912

For the obverse, there is a bust of Liberty facing left with coronet on which is inscribed **LIBERTY**. Back of the coronet and sticking in her hair is an arrangement of agricultural products, including several heads of wheat, bolls of cotton and cotton leaves. Thirteen stars are on the outer edge of the coin with date underneath the bust.

For the 1883 reverse, **UNITED STATES OF AMERICA** is in circular arrangement around outer edge. The Roman numeral "V" is within an open wreath of cotton and corn. At the bottom of the wreath, close to the bow knot, are tiny ears of corn. **E PLURIBUS UNUM** is in very small letters underneath the wreath. There is no denomination.

For the 1883-1912 reverse, **E PLURIBUS UNUM** is in small letters above the wreath of cotton and corn; the word, **CENTS**, is underneath the wreath. Otherwise, the design is unchanged. For 1912, there are mint marks "D" and "S" to be found on the reverse about halfway between the "U" of United and "C" of the word, Cents.

FAIR

Coin will be identified as a Liberty nickel five-cent with the date faint.

ABOUT GOOD

Date will be plain with all lettering on reverse faint.

NICKEL FIVE CENTS

GOOD

Head of Liberty must be well outlined but need not show detail. All letters in legend on reverse must be plain and readable. There will be no **LIBERTY** on the coronet. **E PLURIBUS UNUM** will be faint.

VERY GOOD

Any three letters of **LIBERTY** on coronet must show although they will be worn considerably.

FINE

All letters in **LIBERTY** on coronet will be readable. The letter "I" in **LIBERTY** must show.

[54]

NICKEL FIVE CENTS

VERY FINE

All seven letters in word LIBERTY on coronet must be strong, including the letter "I."

EXTREMELY FINE

There will be a full LIBERTY on the coronet with all letters including the letter "I," very bold. On the reverse, there must be a partial showing of grains on ears of corn at bottom of the wreath.

ABOUT UNCIRCULATED

There must be a full LIBERTY on coronet with all letters very bold. Only a faint trace of wear will show on all hair detail. Practically all grains on ears of corn at bottom of wreath must show.

Special Notation: Genuine 1913 Liberty Head nickels were never placed in circulation or lost to be found. Fake 1913 Liberty Head nickels are made from 1910 and 1911 issues.

NICKEL FIVE CENTS — Buffalo, 1913-1938

For the obverse, the head of an Indian faces right with feathers in hair and braids tied with a string. LIBERTY is at the upper right of field near rim. Date is at lower left below Indian's neck.

For the 1913 Type I reverse, a bison stands on a mound of earth, facing left. UNITED STATES OF AMERICA is around top edge of field. In very small letters, E PLURIBUS UNUM to the right of the bison's hump. Denomination, FIVE CENTS, is under raised ground. Mint marks, if any, are under denomination.

For the 1913-1938 Type II reverse, the bison stands on a straight line with only a slight rise of ground indicated. Otherwise, there is no change.

FAIR

Coin will be identified as to date, mint mark (if any) and type.

ABOUT GOOD

Date will be very weak but it must be readable. Coin will be identified as a Buffalo nickel.

NICKEL FIVE CENTS

GOOD

There will be no horn on the buffalo on reverse although sometimes a short stub of a horn may show. Date and all legends and mottoes must be readable.

VERY GOOD

There will be a full half horn on the buffalo.

FINE

There will be at least a two-thirds full horn on the buffalo. There should be a good rim on the obverse.

NICKEL FIVE CENTS

VERY FINE

There will be a full horn on the buffalo with the last one-third of the horn worn but plain. There will be considerable wear on the Indian's cheek bone. The fork in the brush of the tail will be worn away.

EXTREMELY FINE

There must be a full horn on the buffalo with the last one-third very strong. Ribbon around Indian's braid will show only slight wear.

ABOUT UNCIRCULATED

There must be a full horn with the tip sharp. Only a trace of wear will show on the brush of the buffalo's tail, hair on buffalo's shoulder and the Indian's cheek bone.

NICKEL FIVE CENTS

Special Notation: For some issues of this coin, it is possible that only two-thirds of a full horn will show on the reverse although on the obverse there will be only a faint trace of wear on the Indian's cheek bone, the ribbon around the braid and the hair itself. This is due to a poor strike on the reverse. Coins must be graded, in the main, from conditions on the obverse, but it is best to consult an expert.

On nickels of 1913 (all types) the word **LIBERTY** is poorly struck even on uncirculated specimens. Therefore, **LIBERTY** cannot be used as a grading point.

The surest way to recognize a genuine 3-legged Buffalo Nickel is to examine the hind legs. The hind legs on the genuine specimen have a "moth-eaten" appearance and are not fully rounded.

NICKEL FIVE CENTS — Jefferson, 1938 to Date

For the obverse, there is a portrait of Thomas Jefferson facing left. Motto, **IN GOD WE TRUST,** is on the left edge of field; LIBERTY and date are at the right edge of field.

For the reverse, the main device is a portrait of Jefferson's home, Monticello. **E PLURIBUS UNUM** is in upper field; word, **MONTICELLO,** is immediately below house and **UNITED STATES OF AMERICA** is in lower field. Denomination, **FIVE CENTS,** is beneath **MONTICELLO.** Mint marks (if any) are to lower right of house.

FAIR
Not collectable.

ABOUT GOOD
The rim will be worn down into the lettering on the edge of both the obverse and reverse.

GOOD

The obverse will have a good rim. On the reverse, the rim will be worn down almost to the top of the lettering above Monticello. The four pillars will be practically gone.

NICKEL FIVE CENTS

← *VERY GOOD*

On the reverse, the second pillar from the right will be practically gone; all other three pillars will show.

FINE →

On reverse, the second pillar from right will show but be weak, especially at the bottom.

VERY FINE

On reverse, the lines of the second pillar from the right will not be broken at the top or bottom and will be complete on both sides.

EXTREMELY FINE

On the reverse, the base of the triangle above the four pillars must show although weakly.

ABOUT UNCIRCULATED

On reverse, the base of the triangle above the four pillars must be very plain with very little wear.

NICKEL FIVE CENTS

THREE CENT — Silver, 1851-1873

1851-1853

For the obverse of these dates, a plain edged six-pointed star with small heraldic shield in center is the main device. In the center of each point of the star is a ridge with a raised effect from each edge of the point to the ridge. Single points of the star point to the top and bottom of the coin. Date is at bottom; UNITED STATES OF AMERICA is at top.

For the reverse, a large letter "C" encloses Roman numeral III. On the "C" are circular and diamond designs. Enclosing the two and around the edge of the coin are thirteen small six-pointed stars. Mint mark for 1851-O is just to the right of the numeral III.

1854-1858

For the obverse of these dates, the design is the same except the star is bordered by three raised lines.

For the reverse, the design is the same except an olive sprig has been added above the numeral III and a bundle of three arrows beneath the numeral.

1859-1873

For the obverse of these dates, the design is the same except the star is bordered by two raised lines.

For the reverse, the design is the same as for the preceding type.

FAIR

Not collectable.

ABOUT GOOD

Coin will be identified as Silver Three-Cent piece with date.

←   ### GOOD

Star on obverse will be worn smooth but letters in legend around star as well as date must show plainly. Rim can be worn in spots.

VERY GOOD   →

Date and letters in legend around star must show plainly. There must be a complete rim for both obverse and reverse. Shield within the star must be completely outlined.

THREE CENTS — Silver

FINE

Ridge on top of each point of star will be worn smooth but all six points must show raised effect from outside edge of point to center.

VERY FINE

Ridges on top of points of star will show but they will be worn in places.

EXTREMELY FINE

Ridges on top of points of star must show plainly and be complete on at least five of the six points. However, slight wear exists.

ABOUT UNCIRCULATED

Ridges on top of points of star must show distinctly on at least five of the six points. Only a slight wear will show on Roman numeral III on reverse.

Special Notation: Because of the smallness and the design of the coin, there will be wear on even **EXTREMELY FINE** specimens. Although **UNCIRCULATED** Silver Three-Cent pieces are supposed to show no wear on all six points, sometimes one side of a coin will be struck bolder than the other side. Coins of the 1854, 1855 and 1858 issues are very poorly struck. Uncirculated specimens of these issues will show weak dates on most coins.

HALF DIME — Liberty With Flowing Hair, 1794-1795

For the obverse, head of Liberty faces right with flowing hair unrestrained. LIBERTY is above the head with stars on either side. Date is underneath the bust.

For the reverse, small unrealistic eagle with wings poised for flight and head turned to right is main device. The whole is enclosed in a wreath of laurel. UNITED STATES OF AMERICA is around wreath.

FAIR

Coin will be identified as to date and type.

ABOUT GOOD

Rim on reverse will be worn down into top of letters of legend.

GOOD

Bust on obverse, eagle and wreath on reverse are outlined but will show no detail. All lettering and date must be readable.

HALF DIMES

VERY GOOD

Major facial details for Liberty will show. All lettering on reverse must be plain but will be worn.

← FINE

Ends of Liberty's hair strands will be visible with little detail. Top of hair above forehead will be outlined but worn smooth. All other hair detail will be worn smooth.

VERY FINE →

Top of Liberty's hair above forehead will be worn slightly. Hair on side of head will show some detail.

EXTREMELY FINE

Hair below head and down neck of Liberty will be well defined but will show some wear.

ABOUT UNCIRCULATED

Hair roll above Liberty's forehead will show only slight wear. Facial features will be very plain and hair will be well defined.

HALF DIMES — Draped Bust - Small and Heraldic Eagle, 1796-1805

For the obverse, draped bust of Liberty faces right with flowing hair bound by fillet or ribbon. LIBERTY is at the top of the coin with varying number of stars to right and left. Date is underneath the bust.

For the small eagle reverse, the main device is a small unrealistic eagle poised for flight within a wreath of laurel on left and palm branch on right. UNITED STATES OF AMERICA is around the wreath.

For the large eagle reverse, there is a heraldic eagle with upraised wings as the main device. There is a shield on eagle's breast and his beak carries a scroll on which is inscribed, E PLURIBUS UNUM. Right talon carries bundle of 13 arrows; left talon, an olive branch. There are thirteen stars above the eagle with a circle of clouds above the stars. UNITED STATES OF AMERICA is at top.

FAIR

Coin will be identified as to date and type.

ABOUT GOOD

Rim on reverse will be worn down into top of letters on legend. Date, stars and LIBERTY on obverse must show.

HALF DIMES

GOOD

Liberty's bust on obverse will be fairly well outlined but show no details. Date must be readable.

VERY GOOD

Only the deepest folds at the bottom of Liberty's draped bust will show. All other drapery lines will be worn smooth. Hair from Liberty's forehead down past ear and neck will be worn smooth. Curls at end of hair will be outlined.

FINE

All drapery lines on Liberty's bust will show but not be sharp. Hair from Liberty's forehead past ear and down neck will be outlined but show only slight detail.

VERY FINE

Drapery lines from a point just left of breast cleavage to point halfway around to left will show only slight wear. From there on to hair curls, the drapery will be worn about smooth.

EXTREMELY FINE

All lines in drapery of Liberty's bust will show distinctly around the hair curls. Hair will be well outlined and show details.

ABOUT UNCIRCULATED

Only a trace of wear will show on the highest portions of obverse and reverse. These points will include hair above Liberty's forehead, the shoulder and bust.

HALF DIMES — Capped Bust, 1829-1837

For the obverse there is a capped bust of Liberty with broad ribbon across front of head; on this ribbon is **LIBERTY**. Ringlets of hair protrude from cap above forehead and at ear. Hair falls to shoulders in curls. Date is underneath bust. Stars are on either side of bust.

For the reverse, a heraldic eagle with shield on breast is main device. Above eagle is scroll with motto, **E PLURIBUS UNUM**. Denomination is below eagle.

FAIR

Coin will be identified as to date and type.

HALF DIMES

ABOUT GOOD

Rim will be worn down into top of letters on reverse and stars on obverse. Date will be readable.

GOOD

Date together with all letters in legends and stars must show. Bust of Liberty will be outlined but there will be little or no detail.

VERY GOOD

At least any three letters of word LIBERTY in headband must be readable. All letters in legend and mottoes as well as date must be plain.

FINE

There must be a partial rim for both obverse and reverse. Full LIBERTY on headband must show. Ear will be plain and clasp on left shoulder will show faintly.

HALF DIMES

VERY FINE

There must be a full rim for both obverse and reverse. **LIBERTY** on headband must show plainly. Ear must be distinct and clasp on left shoulder will show plainly.

EXTREMELY FINE

LIBERTY on headband must be very sharp. Ear must be very distinct and clasp on left shoulder must show very plainly. Eyebrow and hair above eye must be well defined. Rest of curls of hair must show considerable detail.

ABOUT UNCIRCULATED

There will be a trace of wear on hair, especially above the eye and the drapery around the front of Liberty's bust.

HALF DIME — Liberty Seated (All Varieties), 1837-1873

1837-1838-O   **1838-1860**

For the obverse of these dates, Liberty is seated with head turned left. Right hand supports a shield on which is a scroll with word, **LIBERTY**. Left hand holds a pole with Liberty Cap atop. Field is plain; date is underneath seated Liberty.

For the reverse, denomination is inside laurel wreath around which is **UNITED STATES OF AMERICA**. Mint mark for 1838-O is within wreath on reverse.

HALF DIMES

1838-1860

For the obverse of these dates, the design is the same as for preceding type except thirteen stars in circular arrangement have been added around Liberty seated.

For the reverse, the design is the same as for preceding type. Mint marks are within the wreath on reverse.

1860-1873

For the obverse of these dates, the design is the same as for preceding types except the legend, UNITED STATES OF AMERICA, replaces the thirteen stars.

For the reverse, the denomination is within a wreath of corn, cotton, wheat and tobacco. Mint marks are on reverse, either within or below wreath.

Note: Grading of Liberty Seated Half Dimes is the same for all types.

FAIR

Coin will be identified as to date, type and denomination although worn considerably.

ABOUT GOOD

Rim will be worn down into top of letters on reverse from 1837-1860 and on obverse from 1860-1873.

GOOD

LIBERTY on shield will be worn smooth but date and legend letters must be plain.

HALF DIMES

→ *VERY GOOD*

There must be a good rim for both obverse and reverse. Any three letters in LIBERTY on shield must show.

FINE →

All seven letters of word LIBERTY on shield must show although letters "L" and "I" will be weak.

← *VERY FINE*

All seven letters of word LIBERTY on shield must be very plain, including the letters "L" and "I."

EXTREMELY FINE →

There must be a complete LIBERTY on shield. Top and bottom edges of scroll on which LIBERTY is located must be raised. Round clasp on Liberty's right shoulder will show faintly.

← *ABOUT UNCIRCULATED*

Only a trace of wear will show on Liberty's knee caps and right shoulder; there will be just a trace of wear at edge of Liberty's hairline.

DIME — Draped Bust Small and Large Eagle, 1796-1807

For the obverse, the draped bust of Liberty faces right with flowing hair bound by a fillet or ribbon. LIBERTY is at top of the coin with varying number of stars to right and left. Date is underneath the bust.

For the small eagle reverse, there is a small unrealistic eagle poised for flight with a wreath of laurel branch on left and palm branch on right. UNITED STATES OF AMERICA is around wreath.

For the large eagle reverse, the main device is a heraldic eagle with upraised wings. A shield is on the eagle's breast and his beak carries a scroll on which is inscribed E PLURIBUS UNUM. There are thirteen stars above eagle with a circle of clouds above stars. UNITED STATES OF AMERICA in circular arrangement at top.

FAIR

Coin will be identified as to date and type although worn considerably.

ABOUT GOOD

Rim on reverse will be worn down into top of letters of legend. Date, stars and LIBERTY on obverse must be identifiable.

DIMES

GOOD

Liberty's bust on obverse will be fairly well outlined but will show no detail. Date and **LIBERTY** must be readable.

VERY GOOD

Only the deepest folds at the bottom of Liberty's draped bust will show. All other drapery lines will be worn smooth. Hair from Liberty's forehead down past ear and down neck will be outlined but show only slight detail.

FINE

Most drapery lines on Liberty's bust will show but not be sharp. Hair from Liberty's forehead past ear and down neck will be outlined but show only slight detail.

VERY FINE

Drapery lines from point just left of breast cleavage to point halfway around to left will show only slight wear. From there to hair curls, the drapery will be about smooth.

DIMES

All lines in drapery on Liberty's bust will show distinctly around to hair curls. On worn dies, these will not show so well. Hair will be well outlined and show detail.

ABOUT UNCIRCULATED

Only a trace of wear will show on the highest portions of obverse and reverse. These points will include hair above forehead, Liberty's shoulder and bust on obverse.

DIME — Capped Bust, 1809-1837

For the obverse, capped bust of Liberty with broad ribbon across front of head faces left. On ribbon is word **LIBERTY**. Ringlets of hair protrude from cap above forehead and at ear. Hair falls to shoulders in curls. Date is underneath bust. Stars on either side of bust. There are many varieties as to size of date, denomination, etc.

For the reverse, a heraldic eagle with shield on breast is main device. Above eagle is scroll with motto, **E PLURIBUS UNUM**. Denomination is below eagle.

FAIR

Coin will be identified as to date and type although worn considerably.

DIMES

ABOUT GOOD

Partial wear will show into lettering on reverse and stars on obverse. Date will be readable.

GOOD

Date together with all letters in legend and mottoes must show. Bust of Liberty will be outlined but there will be little or no detail.

VERY GOOD

At least any three letters of word LIBERTY on headband must be readable. All letters in legend and mottoes and the date must be plain.

FINE

There may be a partial rim for both obverse and reverse. Full LIBERTY on headband must show. Ear will be plain and clasp on left shoulder will be outlined only faintly.

DIMES

VERY FINE

There must be a rim for both obverse and reverse. LIBERTY on headband must show plainly. Ear will be distinct and clasp on left shoulder will show very plainly. On some strikes the rim may not be complete.

EXTREMELY FINE

There will be a sharp LIBERTY on headband, the edges of which must be well defined. The ear will be very distinct. Clasp on left shoulder must be plain. Eyebrow and hair above eye must be well defined. Rest of curls in hair must show considerable detail.

ABOUT UNCIRCULATED

Only a trace of wear on Liberty's hair, especially above the eye and the drapery around the front of Liberty's bust will show.

DIME — Liberty Seated (All Varieties), 1837-1891

1873-1838-O

For the obverse of these dates, Liberty is seated with head turned left. Right hand supports a shield on which is a scroll with word LIBERTY. Her left hand holds a pole with Liberty Cap atop. Field is plain; date is underneath seated Liberty.

For the reverse, denomination is inside laurel wreath around which is UNITED STATES OF AMERICA.

DIMES

1838-1860

For the obverse of these dates, the design is the same as for preceding type except thirteen stars in circular arrangement have been added around Liberty seated.

For the reverse, design is same as for preceding type. Mint marks on reverse either within or below wreath.

1860-1891

For the obverse of these years, the design is the same as for preceding types except the legend, UNITED STATES OF AMERICA, replaces the thirteen stars.

For the reverse, the denomination is within a wreath of corn, cotton, wheat and tobacco. Mint marks are on reverse either within or below the wreath.

FAIR

Coin will be identified as to date and type but worn badly.

ABOUT GOOD

Rim will be worn down into the top of letter of legend on reverse of 1837-1860; for the obverse, 1860-1891.

DIMES

GOOD

LIBERTY on shield will be worn smooth but date and all letters in legend must be plain.

VERY GOOD

Rim on obverse and reverse must be fairly well raised. Any three letters of word LIBERTY on shield must show.

DIMES

FINE

All seven letters of word **LIBERTY** on shield must show although the letters "L" and "I" will be weak.

VERY FINE

All seven letters of word **LIBERTY** on shield must show with the letters "L" and "I" strong.

EXTREMELY FINE

There must be a bold **LIBERTY** on shield. Top and bottom edges of the scroll on which **LIB-ERTY** is located must be very distinct. Round clasp on Liberty's right shoulder must be visible although faint. On some issues the clasp did not strike up so well.

ABOUT UNCIRCULATED

There will be a trace of wear on Liberty's knee caps and right shoulder. Clasp on right shoulder must be very distinct.

DIME — Barber, 1892-1916

For the obverse, classic head of Liberty faces right; she wears a Phrygian cap, symbolic of free men. Laurel wreath encircles head with ends of wreath tied with ribbons. Small fillet above forehead bears word LIBERTY. Legend, UNITED STATES OF AMERICA, is around outer edge of field. Date is underneath bust.

For the reverse, the denomination, ONE DIME, is enclosed within a wreath of corn, cotton, wheat and tobacco. Mint marks are on the reverse just below the bottom of wreath.

FAIR

Coin will be identified as to date and type although worn badly.

ABOUT GOOD

Rim will be worn down into top of letters on obverse.

GOOD

LIBERTY on headband will be worn off but date and all letters in legend must be plain and readable.

VERY GOOD

Any three letters of word LIBERTY on headband must be readable.

DIMES

FINE

Although weak, all seven letters of word **LIBERTY**, including the letter "Y," must show.

VERY FINE

All seven letters of word **LIBERTY** on headband must stand out very plainly. Edges of ribbon not very plain.

EXTREMELY FINE

All seven letters of word **LIBERTY** on headband must be sharp. Top and bottom edges of ribbon on which **LIBERTY** is located must be well defined.

ABOUT UNCIRCULATED

There will be only a trace of wear on Liberty's cheek, top of forehead just above ribbon and hair above her eye. Only slight wear will show on wreath and bow of ribbon on reverse.

[82]

DIME — Winged Liberty (Mercury), 1916-1945

For the reverse, a head of Liberty wearing a winged cap faces left. Wide-spaced **LIBERTY** is around head. **IN GOD WE TRUST**, in very small letters, is to the left of Liberty's neck. Date is to the right of the neck and slightly lower than motto.

For the reverse, the main device is the fasces and olive branch, symbolic of authority and peace. The denomination, **ONE DIME**, is below the fasces. **UNITED STATES OF AMERICA** is around outer edge of coin. **E PLURIBUS UNUM** is in smaller letters in lower right field. Mint marks are to the left of the lower end of olive branch.

FAIR

Coin will be identified as to date, mint mark (if any) and type.

ABOUT GOOD

Rim will be worn down into top of letters of obverse and reverse.

GOOD

Fasces on reverse should be outlined well although the sticks and the diagonal bands will be worn away. All letters in legends and mottoes as well as date and mint mark (if any) must be plain.

DIMES

VERY GOOD

At least one-third of the sticks in the fasces bundle must show.

FINE →

Although worn, the two diagonal bands must show and come to the center of the bundle of sticks. One or both bands will be worn smooth at the midpoint for a distance that is approximately the width of a stick. All vertical lines in the bundle must show.

VERY FINE

The two diagonal bands must show where they cross the bundle of sticks. Liberty's hair braid will show considerable detail.

EXTREMELY FINE

The two diagonal bands must show and be raised where they cross the center of the bundle of sticks. Liberty's hair braid across the head must be sharp and show details as well as hair in front of ear.

DIMES

ABOUT
UNCIRCULATED

Only a trace of wear will show on the two diagonal bands. Bands must be raised and very bold. Only a trace of wear will show on Liberty's hair above the forehead and in front of ear.

Special Notation: Coins of this issue classified as GOOD must show a plain date. If the rim has been worn into the date, the coin cannot be classified as GOOD or better. Rare coins of this issue — 1916-D, 1917-D, 1921, 1921-D, 1926-S and 1927-D — are often overgraded but incorrectly so.

Dimes of 1921 and 1921-D are difficult to grade by this system. Grading must be done principally by the obverse, ignoring the reverse. Dates with a poor "1" and obverses as a whole poorly struck are not desirable. Well struck dimes of this date have a greater market value.

For all scarce dates of this issue with mint marks, be sure to check mint marks very carefully for fakes. Check not only the mint mark itself but the corresponding position on the obverse side of the dime.

DIME — Roosevelt, 1946 to Date

For the obverse, there is the portrait of Franklin D. Roosevelt facing left with LIBERTY in large letters on outer edge of coin in front of face. IN GOD WE TRUST in very small letters is to the left of neck and date to right.

For the reverse, the torch of Liberty between sprays of oak and laurel is the main device. E PLURIBUS UNUM is in straight line across torch and sprays. ONE DIME is below torch. UNITED STATES OF AMERICA is around the outer edge at top.

FAIR

Not collectable.

ABOUT GOOD

Not collectable.

DIMES

GOOD

There must be a slight rim for both obverse and reverse. Hairlines on head will be worn smooth. Torch and flame will be outlined but worn smooth. Date, legends and mottoes must be readable.

VERY GOOD

Vertical lines on torch will show faintly on the sides with the center smooth. Horizontal lines on torch will be smooth. Very few distinct hairlines will show but all letters and date must be plain.

FINE

Flame of torch will be worn smooth. Horizontal lines on torch will not show detail but all vertical lines on torch will show.

DIMES

VERY FINE

Some lines will show in flame of torch. All horizontal lines on torch will show but be worn. All vertical lines on torch must be plain. Most of hairlines on Roosevelt's head will show plainly.

EXTREMELY FINE

Flame of torch will be well defined and detailed. All horizontal and vertical lines on torch will show very plainly. All hairlines on Roosevelt's head will show only slight wear.

ABOUT UNCIRCULATED

There will be a trace of wear on lines of flame of torch and on Roosevelt's hair just above the ear.

Special Notation: Dimes of these years on which the rim has worn into the date are not collectable.

DIMES

TWENTY CENT — Liberty Seated, 1875-1878

For the obverse, Liberty, wearing a Greek chiton with neck and arms bare, is seated on a rock. The head is turned to the left. She holds a pole in her left hand. On top of the pole is the Liberty Cap. Her right hand supports the shield of the United States which rests on the ground. Across the shield is a scroll on which is inscribed LIBERTY.

For the reverse, main device is an eagle with wings outstretched and inverted; an olive branch is in the left talon and three arrows in the right. Below eagle is denomination, TWENTY CENTS. Above eagle in circular arrangement the legend, UNITED STATES OF AMERICA. Edge of coin is plain without reeding.

FAIR

Coin will be identified as to denomination, date and type.

ABOUT GOOD

There will be partial wear into top of letters on reverse. The date will be faint.

GOOD

LIBERTY on shield will be worn smooth but date and all letters in legends must be plain.

[89]

TWENTY-CENT PIECES

←   *VERY GOOD*

Rim on obverse and reverse must be fairly well raised. Any three letters of word LIBERTY on shield must show.

FINE   →

All seven letters of word LIBERTY on shield must show although the letters "L" and "I" will be weak.

←   *VERY FINE*

All seven letters of word LIBERTY on shield must show with the letters "L" and "I" strong. Edges of scroll will be worn.

EXTREMELY FINE   →

Complete LIBERTY on shield must be sharp. Bottom and top edges of scroll on which LIBERTY is located must be raised and sharp. Round clasp on Liberty's right shoulder must show plainly, but will show slight wear.

ABOUT UNCIRCULATED

There will be a trace of wear on Liberty's kneecaps, arms and hair. Lines of her garments must be very bold. Outline of clasp on right shoulder must be

raised. Only slight wear will show on eagle's breast on reverse.

QUARTER DOLLAR — Draped Bust - Small Eagle, 1796

For the obverse, a draped bust of Liberty faces right with long, loose hair. Two side locks are drawn back and held with a ribbon. Stars in circular arrangement to right and left of LIBERTY at top. Date is underneath the bust.

For the reverse, wreath composed of laurel leaves on left and palm leaves on right enclose a small, unrealistic eagle with wings poised for flight. UNITED STATES OF AMERICA is in circular arrangement around outer edge of coin.

FAIR

Coin will be identified as to date and type although worn badly.

ABOUT GOOD

Rim on reverse will be worn down into top of letters of legend. Date, stars and LIBERTY on obverse must show although worn.

GOOD

Eagle on reverse and Liberty's bust on obverse will be outlined but show no details. Some leaves of the wreath on reverse will show faintly. Date and all lettering must be plain.

QUARTER DOLLARS

VERY GOOD

Only the deepest folds at the bottom of Liberty's draped bust will show. All other drapery lines will be smooth. Hair from forehead down past ear and neck will be worn smooth. Curls at the end of hair will be outlined.

FINE

Some drapery lines on Liberty's bust will show but not be sharp. Hair from forehead past ear and down neck will be outlined but show only few details.

VERY FINE

Drapery lines from point just left of breast cleavage to point halfway around to left will show only slight wear. From there on to hair curls, the drapery will be worn smooth.

EXTREMELY FINE

All lines in drapery on Liberty's bust will show distinctly around to hair curls. Hair will be well outlined and detailed.

ABOUT UNCIRCULATED

Only a faint trace of wear will show on the highest portions of the obverse and reverse: hair above forehead, shoulder and bust; breast of eagle.

QUARTER DOLLAR — Draped Bust - Heraldic Eagle, 1804-1807

For the obverse, the design is the same as for the 1796 quarter dollar.
For the reverse, the main device is a heraldic eagle with large shield on breast. Right talon grasps thirteen arrows; left talon, an olive branch. In eagle's beak is a scroll on which is inscribed E PLURIBUS UNUM. Above eagle's head are thirteen stars beneath an arch of clouds. Legend, UNITED STATES OF AMERICA, in circular arrangement around outer edge of field. Denomination is underneath the eagle.

FAIR

Coin will be identified as to date and type although worn badly.

ABOUT GOOD

Rim on reverse will be worn down into top of letters of legend. Date, stars and LIBERTY on obverse must show.

GOOD

All of motto, E PLURIBUS UNUM, will be worn away. All other lettering and the date must be plain.

QUARTER DOLLARS

VERY GOOD

There will be a partial showing of the motto, E PLURIBUS UNUM, on reverse. Only the deepest folds of Liberty's draped bust will show. All other drapery lines will be worn smooth. Hair from forehead past ear and down neck will be worn smooth.

FINE

Some drapery lines on Liberty's bust will show but will not be sharp. Hair from forehead, past ear and down neck will be outlined but show only slight detail.

VERY FINE

Drapery lines from point just left of breast cleavage to point halfway around to the left will show only slight wear. From there on to hair curls, the drapery will be worn smooth.

EXTREMELY FINE

All lines in drapery on Liberty's bust will show distinctly around to hair curls. Hair will be well outlined and detailed.

ABOUT UNCIRCULATED

There will be only a trace of wear on the very highest points: hair above the forehead, drapery on Liberty's bust and shoulder; eagle's head and ribbon on which is inscribed E PLURIBUS UNUM; tail feather of the eagle.

Special Notation: On some specimens, the motto, E PLURIBUS UNUM, is not struck up as sharply as others.

QUARTER DOLLAR — Capped Bust, 1815-1828

For the obverse, there is a large draped bust of Liberty facing left with loose falling hair about neck and shoulders. Liberty Cap is on her head, the band of the cap inscribed with LIBERTY. Stars on the outer edge of the coin; date is below bust.

For the reverse, legend, UNITED STATES OF AMERICA, is around outer edge. Main device is an eagle with outstretched and inverted wings; heraldic shield is on eagle's breast. Eagle holds olive branch in right talon and three arrows in left. Below eagle is denomination. Above eagle's head is scroll on which is inscribed E PLURIBUS UNUM.

FAIR

Coin will be identified as to type and date but will be worn badly.

ABOUT GOOD

Rim will be worn down into top of letters on reverse and stars on obverse.

GOOD

Letters in legend and motto on reverse, date and stars on obverse will be plain. There will be a faint trace of LIBERTY on turban. Bust of Liberty will be well outlined but there may be few details.

VERY GOOD

At least any three letters of word **LIBERTY** on cap must show plainly. Clasp on left shoulder will be visible.

FINE

There will be considerable wear on hair, especially above Liberty's eye. Clasp on shoulder must be plain. There will be a full **LIBERTY** on headband showing plainly. E PLURIBUS UN-UM on reverse must show plainly.

VERY FINE

There will be little wear on Liberty's hair. Hairline above Liberty's eye must show plainly. Clasp on left shoulder must be distinct.

EXTREMELY FINE

Hair will be well defined and sharp. Although the center will be worn smooth, clasp on Liberty's left shoulder must be bold. Eyebrow must be well defined as well as hair above eye and just under cap.

ABOUT UNCIRCULATED

Only a faint trace of wear will show on hair. Details of clasp – resembling letter "W" in center – must be clear and bold. Only a faint trace of wear must show on toes and claws of eagle and arrows on reverse.

QUARTER DOLLAR — Capped Bust, 1831-1838

For the obverse, the design for these years is the same as previous issue except that the size of the coin and size of Liberty's bust are reduced.

For the reverse, the design for these years is the same as for 1815-1828 except there is no scroll and motto above the eagle.

FAIR

Coin will be identified as to date and type but will be worn badly.

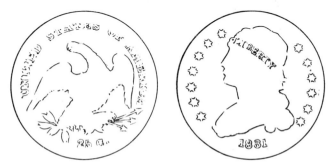

ABOUT GOOD

Lettering on reverse will not be complete. Balance of coin will be in good condition.

GOOD

There must be a slight rim for both obverse and reverse. Stars, date and letters in legends must be plain and readable. Bust of Liberty will be well outlined but hair above eye and ear will be worn smooth. There will be no details on cap.

QUARTER DOLLARS

VERY GOOD

There will be a well developed rim for obverse and reverse. Major details of cap and garments must show but will be worn considerably. There will be a full **LIBERTY** on turban. Clasp on left shoulder will be plain but worn. Hair above Liberty's eye will be worn almost smooth.

FINE

Cap will be detailed with some spots worn almost smooth. Clasp on left shoulder will be distinct. All lines of hair must show with some detail. Drapery on front of bust will be worn with some details.

VERY FINE

Clasp on left shoulder will be sharp. Only slight wear will show on lines of cap. Liberty's ear must be distinct with all lines present. All hair details will show with evidence of wear.

EXTREMELY FINE

All hair details must be bold. Clasp on left shoulder will be bold. Ear will be sharp with all lines raised. Only a slight amount of wear will show on lines of garment around Liberty's bust.

QUARTER DOLLARS

ABOUT UNCIRCULATED

Only very slight wear will show on stars, hair and top of cap. Only a trace of wear will show on eagle's claws and arrows on reverse.

QUARTER DOLLAR — Liberty Seated (All Varieties), 1838-1891

1838-1865

For the obverse, Liberty, wearing a Greek chiton with neck and arms bare, is seated on a rock. The head is turned to the observer's left. She holds in her left hand a pole atop of which is the Liberty Cap. Her right hand supports the shield of the United States. Across the shield is a scroll on which is lettered **LIBERTY**. Stars are on outer edge of coin on each side of head. Arrows by the side of the date 1853-55 issues denote reduction in weight of coin; arrows by the side of the date in the 1873-74 issues denote increase in weight of coins.

For the reverse, main device is an eagle with shield on breast. Eagle's wings are outstretched and inverted. Right talon grasps an olive branch; left talon, three arrows. Denomination is below eagle. **UNITED STATES OF AMERICA** is in circular arrangement on outer edge of coin. For the date 1853, there are rays around the eagle. Mint marks will be under eagle on reverse.

1866-1891

The obverse is the same as for the 1838-1865 issues; on the reverse, a scroll was added with motto, **IN GOD WE TRUST**. Otherwise, the design is the same.

Note: Grading standards are same for both types.

QUARTER DOLLARS

Coin will be identified as to type and date although worn badly.

ABOUT GOOD

The rim will be worn down with some wear into letters of legend on reverse.

GOOD

There must be a slight rim for both obverse and reverse. **LIBERTY** on the shield will be worn smooth but date and letters in legend must be plain and readable.

←   **VERY GOOD**

Rim on obverse and reverse must be fairly well raised. Any three letters of **LIBERTY** on shield must show.

FINE

All seven letters of word **LIBERTY** on shield must show although letters "L" and "I" will be weak.

VERY FINE →

All seven letters of word **LIBERTY** on shield must show with letters "L" and "I" strong. Edges of scroll will show wear.

EXTREMELY FINE

There will be a complete bold **LIBERTY** on shield. Top and bottom edges of scroll on which **LIBERTY** is located must be raised and sharp. Round clasp on Liberty's right shoulder must show plainly, but show slight wear.

QUARTER DOLLARS

*ABOUT
UNCIRCULATED*

There will be only a trace of wear on Liberty's knee caps and arms. Lines of garment must be very sharp. Outline of clasp on Liberty's shoulder must be raised. Liberty's foot must be clearly separated from sandal. There will be only a trace of wear on the eagle's wing tips and head.

QUARTER DOLLAR — Barber, 1892-1916

For the obverse, a large head of Liberty faces right, wearing a Liberty Cap with laurel wreath around head at edge of cap. The ends of the wreath are tied with a ribbon in a bow knot with the two loose ends extending towards the first star. A fillet or ribbon on which is word **LIBERTY** adorns her brow. Above the head is motto, **IN GOD WE TRUST**, with six six-pointed stars to the left and seven to the right. Date is underneath the head.

QUARTER DOLLARS

For the reverse, an eagle is the main device with wings outstretched and extending to outer edges of coin over the legend, **UNITED STATES OF AMERICA**. There is a shield on the eagle's breast; right talon holds an olive branch; left talon, a bundle of thirteen arrows. In the beak of the eagle is a scroll on which is inscribed E PLURIBUS UNUM. Above the head is a galaxy of thirteen five-pointed stars; below the eagle is the denomination. Mint marks are immediately underneath tail of eagle.

FAIR

Coin will be identified as to type and date although worn badly.

ABOUT GOOD →

Rim will be worn down into letters on reverse.

← *GOOD*

LIBERTY on headband will be worn smooth but date and letters in legends must be plain and readable.

VERY GOOD →

At least any three letters of **LIBERTY** on headband must be readable.

← *FINE*

Although weak, all seven letters of word **LIBERTY**, including "Y," on headband must show.

← *VERY FINE*

All seven letters of word **LIBERTY** on headband must be strong. Edges of ribbon will show wear.

EXTREMELY FINE →

All seven letters of word **LIBERTY** on headband must be bold. Top and bottom edges of ribbon on which **LIBERTY** is located must be well defined, but show wear.

ABOUT UNCIRCULATED

There will be a trace of wear only on Liberty's forehead just above the ribbon, cheek and hair above eye. Liberty's cap must show only a trace of wear on the puff. Only a trace of wear will show on eagle's wing tips, head and tail.

QUARTER DOLLAR — Standing Liberty Type I, 1916-1917

QUARTER DOLLARS

For the obverse, the main device is a heroic figure of Liberty, bearing on left arm a shield on which is outlined a smaller shield and an outer border of stars. Liberty's right arm is extended with the hand holding a sprig of olive. Wide-spaced **LIBERTY** is at the top; date is at the bottom. Liberty stands on a pedestal in an opening formed by a wall on either side. Down each side of the wall are five-pointed stars. **IN GOD WE TRUST** is in a divided line at top of wall. For Type I, Liberty is clothed in a flowing garment.

For the reverse, an eagle in full flight is main device. For Type I, the eagle is flying low. **UNITED STATES** is in circular arrangement at top, **OF AMERICA** in two straight lines and motto, **E PLURIBUS UNUM**, between up raised wings of eagle. On outer edge of coin are six five-pointed stars on one side and seven on the other. Denomination is at the bottom underneath eagle. Mint marks are on obverse at left and a little above the date.

FAIR

Not collectable even when date has been brought out by chemicals.

← *ABOUT GOOD*
Date will be barely visible.

GOOD ▶

Top of date will be worn but the date and all lettering will be readable. Liberty's right leg will be worn about smooth. Toes will be worn away. Much wear will be visible on Liberty's left leg and garment lines above hip.

← *VERY GOOD*

There will be a complete date with the top and bottom of the figures standing out distinctly. Although Liberty's right leg will show considerable wear, the toes will show faintly. Garment lines above left leg must be visible.

QUARTER DOLLARS

← FINE

Rounded contour of Liberty's right leg will be worn flat from hip down past knee and through ankle. Toes will show but not be sharp. Left leg at knee cap will show some wear. Garment line above right knee cap will be visible only at sides of leg.

VERY FINE →

Rounded contour of Liberty's right leg will be flattened on the very top from about halfway between hip and knee to ankle. Garment line across right leg at midpoint will be worn on top of leg but will show plainly at sides.

← EXTREMELY FINE

Right breast of Liberty will come to a full round point. There will be slight wear on Liberty's right leg just above knee cap to ankle but toes will be very sharp. Garment line across right leg above knee cap will show. Shield will show slight wear.

ABOUT UNCIRCULATED →

There will be only slight wear on highest point of knee cap. Garment line across right leg above knee cap must be clear and distinct. Shield will show trace of wear.

Special Notation: Fake 1916 Standing Liberty Quarters are made by building up with silver the platform on which Liberty stands and on which date is located. The date is then recut. These fakes are very hard to detect. Therefore, 1916 Liberty Standing Quarters should be bought from a reputable dealer. The Standing Liberty Quarter is one of the most difficult coins to grade, especially those from 1916-1924.

QUARTER DOLLARS

QUARTER DOLLAR — Standing Liberty Type II, 1917-1930

For dates of this type, the design is essentially the same as for Type I except that Liberty wears a breast plate of armor and after 1924, the date is located in a depression in the pedestal.

For the reverse of this type, the design is somewhat the same as for Type I except that the eagle flies higher with three stars underneath. Mint marks located same as for Type I.

1917-1924

FAIR

Not collectable.

ABOUT GOOD

Date will be barely visible.

GOOD

Top of date will be worn but the whole date will be readable. All lettering on reverse must be plain.

QUARTER DOLLARS

VERY GOOD

There will be a complete date with the top and bottom of the figures standing out distinctly. Lettering on reverse must be very plain.

FINE

Rounded contour of Liberty's right leg will be worn flat from hip down past knee and through ankle. Toes will show but not be sharp. Left leg will show wear. Garment line above right knee cap will be visible only at sides of leg.

VERY FINE

Top of Liberty's right leg will show wear from about halfway between hip and knee and down to ankle. Garment line across right leg above knee cap will be worn but show at sides.

EXTREMELY FINE

Only slight wear will show on head and breast of Liberty. There will be slight wear on right leg just above knee cap to ankle but toes of Liberty will be sharp. Only slight wear will show on folds of scarf across Liberty's body.

QUARTER DOLLARS

ABOUT UNCIRCULATED

Only slight wear will show on the highest point of right knee cap. Garment line across right leg above knee cap must be clear and distinct.

Special Notation: All years of the Standing Liberty Quarter Dollar were minted with the so-called "flat head" and "round head" Liberty. Strictly GEM UNCIRCU-LATED Standing Liberty Quarter Dollars will have perfect heads and will command higher prices than the "flat heads." The percentage of "flat heads" in uncirculated conditions runs very high.

1925-1930

FAIR

Not collectable.

ABOUT GOOD

Not collectable.

GOOD

Date, lettering and mint mark (if any) must be plain.

VERY GOOD

Scarf will be worn smooth where it crosses Liberty's body. Armor plate on bosom will be worn smooth. Straps over shoulders must show plainly. There must be a good rim for both obverse and reverse and not worn into date. All letters in legends must stand out plainly.

FINE

There will be considerable wear on both breasts and on scarf where it crosses Liberty's body to shield. Some details of armor will show.

VERY FINE

Details of armor on chest will show very plainly except on top of right breast. Scarf from hand to shield must be complete and well defined.

EXTREMELY FINE

There will be a trace of wear only on the highest part of the scarf and on the tip of the right breast.

ABOUT UNCIRCULATED

There will be slight wear only on the very tip of the right knee cap.

QUARTER DOLLARS

QUARTER DOLLAR — Washington, 1932 to Date

For the obverse, portrait of bewigged Washington faces left. **LIBERTY** is at top in large letters. **IN GOD WE TRUST** is in small letters to the left of the neck. Date is underneath the bust.

For the reverse, realistic eagle with wings, outstretched and inverted stands on bundle of arrows. Immediately above head of eagle in small letters is **E PLURIBUS UNUM.** At top in circular arrangement **UNITED STATES OF AMERICA.** Below arrows are crossed olive branches with tops pointing up and superimposed on lower part of eagle's wings. Denomination is at bottom edge of coin. Mint marks are immediately under the crossed olive branches.

1932 Issue

FAIR

Although badly worn, coin must be identified as to date and mint mark.

ABOUT GOOD

Rim on reverse will be worn down into top of letters. There will be a faint trace of the motto, **IN GOD WE TRUST.**

QUARTER DOLLARS

→ ← **GOOD**

Only a trace of the letters in motto, IN
GOD WE TRUST, will show.

VERY GOOD →

Top of letters on reverse will show some
wear but be plain. About half of the letters
in motto, **IN GOD WE TRUST**, must
show.

← **FINE**

IN GOD WE TRUST must be well defined but will be weak.

VERY FINE

IN GOD WE TRUST must show plainly. Hairlines for top of head will
be worn but details will be plain. Hair in front of and back of ear will be
well defined with hair across ear showing details. Feathers on right and
left side of eagle's breast on reverse will show plainly.

EXTREMELY FINE

Hair in front of, across and back of ear will be sharp with slight wear. Feathers on eagle's breast will be very plain except at the very top. There will be some wear on the very top of eagle's legs.

ABOUT UNCIRCULATED

Only a spot of wear will show on the highest part of hair in front of and back of ear. There will be only a trace of wear on the eagle's breast and legs.

1934 to Date

FAIR

Not collectable.

ABOUT GOOD

Rim on reverse will be worn down into top of letters.

GOOD

There will be a slight rim for both obverse and reverse. Reverse rim will be worn in spots. Head will be well outlined but have no hair detail. Date will be plain.

VERY GOOD

There will be a slight rim for both obverse and reverse with no worn spots. Top of letters will show some wear but be plain. Puff of wig and some hairlines above the puff will show. Tip of right wing of eagle will be well defined but show no details.

QUARTER DOLLARS

FINE

Hairlines for top of head will be worn with few details. Hair in front of and across ear will be well defined but worn considerably. The feathers on eagle's breast will show faintly. Eagle's legs will be worn considerably with few details.

VERY FINE

Hairlines for top of head will be worn but all details will be plain. Hair in front of and back of ear will be well defined with hair across ear showing details. Feathers on right and left sides of eagle's breast will show plainly.

EXTREMELY FINE

Hair in front of, across and back of ear will be sharp with only slight wear. Feathers on eagle's breast except at the very top will be very plain. Some wear will show on top of eagle's legs.

ABOUT UNCIRCULATED

Only a spot of wear will show on the highest part of hair in front of and back of ear. Only a faint trace of wear will show on eagle's breast and legs.

Special Notation: 1937-S Washington Quarters, as a rule, are struck weakly on the reverse.

QUARTER DOLLARS

HALF DOLLARS

HALF DOLLAR — Liberty With Flowing Hair, Small Eagle,

1794-1795

For the obverse, bust of Liberty with long, loose hair faces right. LIB-ERTY is at top with stars in circular arrangement on either side. Date is at the bottom underneath the bust.

For the reverse, UNITED STATES OF AMERICA is around the outer field. Main device is an unrealistic eagle with outstretched wings and standing on a rock. The head of the eagle is turned to the right. Eagle is enclosed in a wreath of laurel branches. On edge of the coin is denomination, FIFTY CENTS OR HALF A DOLLAR.

FAIR

Coin will be identified as to type and date.

ABOUT GOOD

Rim on reverse will be worn down into top of letters.

HALF DOLLARS

GOOD

Bust on obverse, eagle and wreath on reverse are outlined but will have no details. All lettering and date will be readable.

VERY GOOD

Major facial details for Liberty will show. All lettering on reverse will be plain but worn.

← FINE

Ends of Liberty's hair strands will be visible. Top of hair above forehead will be outlined but worn smooth. All other hair details will be worn smooth.

VERY FINE →

Top of Liberty's hair above forehead will be worn slightly. Hair on side of head will show some detail.

HALF DOLLARS

EXTREMELY FINE

Hair below head and down Liberty's neck will be defined and detailed but will show some wear.

ABOUT UNCIRCULATED

Hair roll above Liberty's forehead will show only slight wear. Facial features will be very plain and hair will be well defined.

HALF DOLLAR — Draped Bust, Small Eagle, 1796-1797

For the obverse, draped bust of Liberty faces right with long, loose hair. Two side locks of hair are drawn back and held with ribbon. Stars in circular arrangement to right and left of **LIBERTY** at top. Date is underneath bust.

For the reverse, wreath composed of laurel leaves on left and palm leaves on right encloses eagle similar to 1794-95 half dollar. Below wreath is the fraction "½." **UNITED STATES OF AMERICA** is in circular arrangement around outer edge.

FAIR

Coin will be identified as to type and date.

HALF DOLLARS

ABOUT GOOD

Rim will be worn down into top of letters on reverse. Date, stars and LIBERTY on obverse must show.

GOOD

Liberty's bust on obverse and eagle on reverse will be fairly well outlined but show no details. Some leaves of the wreath will show only faintly. Date must be readable.

VERY GOOD

Only the deepest folds at the bottom of Liberty's bust will show. All other drapery lines will be worn smooth. Hair from forehead down past ear and neck will be worn smooth. Curls at end of hair will be outlined.

FINE

Some drapery lines on Liberty's bust will show but not be sharp. Hair from forehead past ear and down neck will be outlined but show only slight detail.

HALF DOLLARS

VERY FINE

Drapery lines from point just left of breast cleavage to point halfway around to left will show only slight wear. From there on to hair curls, the drapery will be worn smooth.

EXTREMELY FINE

All lines in drapery on Liberty's bust will show distinctly around to hair curls. Hair will be well outlined and detailed.

ABOUT UNCIRCULATED

Only a trace of wear will show on the highest portions of obverse and reverse: hair above the forehead, the shoulder, bust and the breast of the eagle.

HALF DOLLARS

HALF DOLLAR — Draped Bust, Heraldic Eagle, 1801-1807

For the obverse, the design is the same as for the 1796-1797 half dollar.

For the reverse, main device is a heraldic eagle with shield on breast. Right talon grasps thirteen arrows and left, olive branch. In eagle's beak is a scroll on which is inscribed E PLURIBUS UNUM. Above eagle's head are thirteen stars beneath an arch of clouds. Legend, UNITED STATES OF AMERICA, in circular arrangement around outer edge.

FAIR

Coin will be identified as to date and type.

← ABOUT GOOD

Rim will be worn down into top of letters on reverse. Date, stars and LIBERTY on obverse must show.

GOOD →

All of motto, E PLURIBUS UN-UM, will be worn away. All other lettering and the date must be plain.

← VERY GOOD

There will be a partial showing of motto, E PLURIBUS UNUM. Only the deepest folds at the bottom of Liberty's draped bust will show. All other drapery lines will be worn smooth. Hair from forehead down past ear and neck will be worn smooth.

HALF DOLLARS

FINE

Some drapery lines on Liberty's bust will show but not be sharp. Hair from forehead, past ear and down neck will be outlined with only slight details showing.

VERY FINE

Drapery lines from a point just left of breast cleavage to point halfway around to left will show only slight wear. From there on to hair curls, the drapery will be worn smooth.

EXTREMELY FINE

All lines in drapery on Liberty's bust will show distinctly around to hair curls. Hair will be well outlined and detailed.

ABOUT UNCIRCULATED

There will be a trace of wear on the very highest points: hair above forehead, drapery on Liberty's bust and shoulder.

HALF DOLLARS
HALF DOLLAR — Capped Bust, 1807-1836

For the obverse, there is a large draped bust of Liberty facing left with loose falling hair about neck and shoulders. Liberty Cap is on her head; the band of cap is inscribed with word, **LIBERTY**. Stars are on outer edge; date is below the bust.

For the reverse, legend, **UNITED STATES OF AMERICA**, is around outer edge. Main device is an eagle with outstretched and inverted wings; eagle holds olive branch in right talon and three arrows in left. Below eagle is denomination; above eagle is scroll on which is lettered **E PLUR- IBUS UNUM**.

FAIR

Not collectable.

ABOUT GOOD

There will be par- tial wear into let- ters on reverse and stars on obverse. Date will be read- able.

GOOD

Date together with all letters in legends and stars must show. Bust of Liberty will be out- lined but show few or no details.

HALF DOLLARS

VERY GOOD

All of word **LIBERTY** in headband will show but some letters will be faint. All letters in legends and the date must be plain. Clasp on left shoulder will show faintly. Hair curl above clasp will be worn almost smooth.

FINE

Clasp on left shoulder must show plainly. Hair curl above clasp must be well outlined with some detail.

VERY FINE

Clasp on left shoulder will be very plain. Hair curl above clasp will be well defined and show all detail but highest portions will show wear. Hair above eye must show plainly.

EXTREMELY FINE

Clasp on left shoulder must be sharp. Hair curl above clasp will show only trace of wear. Eyebrow and hair above eye must be well defined. Rest of curls must show considerable detail.

HALF DOLLARS

Only a trace of wear will show above Liberty's forehead and just under "L" in LIBERTY. Lines in cap will be sharp with only a trace of wear. Only slight wear will show on drapery around Liberty's bust. There will be slight wear on eagle's talons and arrowheads on reverse.

HALF DOLLAR — Capped Bust, 1836-1839

1836-1837

For the obverse, the design is similar to Capped Bust Half Dollars for 1807-1836. For the reverse, the design is the same for 1807-1836 Half Dollars except the motto above the eagle has been removed and the denomination, 50 **CENTS**, appears underneath the eagle. Edge is reeded.

1838-1839

For the obverse, the design is similar to Capped Bust Half Dollars for 1807-1836. For the reverse, the design is the same as for 1807-1836 Capped Bust Half Dollars except the motto above eagle has been removed and the denomination, **HALF DOL.**, is underneath the eagle. Edge is reeded.

Note: Grading for these two types is the same.

FAIR

Although coin will be worn badly, it will be identified as to type and date.

HALF DOLLARS

← *ABOUT GOOD*

LIBERTY on headband will be worn away. Date and all other lettering must be readable.

GOOD →

There will be a trace of LIBERTY on headband.

← *VERY GOOD*

At least three letters of word LIBERTY on headband must be readable.

FINE →

Full LIBERTY on headband must be plain.

← *VERY FINE*

Full LIBERTY on headband must be sharp. Clasp on shoulder must be distinct.

EXTREMELY FINE →

LIBERTY on headband must be strong. Hair above forehead must show detail.

HALF DOLLARS

Only a trace of wear will show on Liberty's hair above forehead and just under "L" in LIBERTY. Lines in cap will be sharp with only a trace of wear. Only slight wear will show on drapery around Liberty's bust. There will be slight wear on eagle's talons and arrowheads on reverse.

HALF DOLLAR — Liberty Seated (All Varieties), 1839-1891

1839-1866

For the obverse, Liberty, wearing a Greek chiton with neck and arms bare, is seated on a rock. The head is turned to the observer's left. She holds in her left hand a pole atop which is a Liberty Cap. Her right hand supports the shield of the United States. Across the shield is a scroll on which is lettered LIBERTY. Stars on the outer edge of coin to each side of the head; date is underneath the seated figure. Arrows by the side of the date for 1853, 1854 and 1855 to denote a reduction in weight of coin.

For the reverse, main device is an eagle with shield on breast. Eagle's wings are outstretched and inverted. Right talon grasps an olive branch; the left talon, three arrows. Denomination is below eagle. UNITED STATES OF AMERICA is in circular arrangement on outer edge of coin. Rays behind eagle were added only for 1853. Mint marks on reverse under eagle.

HALF DOLLARS

1866-1891

For the obverse, the design is the same as for the years 1839-1866. Arrows by the side of the date were added in 1873 and 1874 to denote an increase in weight of coin. For the reverse, the design is the same as for the years 1839-1866 except that a scroll has been added above the eagle. On the scroll is the motto IN GOD WE TRUST.

Note: Grading is the same for both types.

FAIR

Coin will be identified as to date and type.

ABOUT GOOD

Rim will be worn down into letters on reverse.

← GOOD

There must be a slight rim for both obverse and reverse. LIBERTY on shield will be worn smooth. Date and all letters in legends must be plain and readable.

VERY GOOD →

Rim on obverse and reverse must be fairly well raised. Any three letters of word LIBERTY on shield must show.

HALF DOLLARS

FINE

All seven letters of word **LIBERTY** on shield must show although the letters "L" and "I" will be weak.

VERY FINE

All seven letters of word **LIBERTY** on shield must show with the letters "L" and "I" strong.

EXTREMELY FINE

There will be a complete strong **LIBERTY** on shield. The top and bottom edges of the scroll on which **LIBERTY** is located must be very distinct. Round clasp on Liberty's right shoulder must show plainly.

ABOUT UNCIRCULATED

Only a trace of wear will show on Liberty's knee caps, arms and head. Outline of clasp on Liberty's right shoulder must be raised as well as garment line from clasp to right side of neck. Details of clothes must be very sharp. Liberty's foot must be clearly separated from her sandal. Only a trace of wear will show on eagle's neck and wing tips.

HALF DOLLARS

HALF DOLLAR — Barber, 1892-1915

For the obverse, a large head of Liberty faces to the right. She wears a Liberty Cap with a laurel wreath around the edge of the cap. The ends of the wreath are tied with a ribbon in a bow knot with the two loose ends extending towards the first star. A fillet or ribbon on which is word LIBERTY adorns her brow. Above the head is the motto, IN GOD WE TRUST, with six six-pointed stars to the left and seven to the right. Date is underneath the neck.

For the reverse, an eagle is the main device with wings outstretched and extending to the outer edges and over the legend, UNITED STATES OF AMERICA. There is a shield on the eagle's breast; right talon holds an olive branch with thirteen leaves; the left talon, a bundle of thirteen arrows. In the eagle's beak is a scroll on which is inscribed E PLURIBUS UNUM. Above the head is a galaxy of thirteen five-pointed stars. Below the eagle is the denomination. Mint marks are immediately below the tail of the eagle.

FAIR

Coin will be identified as to type and date although badly worn.

ABOUT GOOD

Rim will be worn down into letters on reverse. Date must be visible.

HALF DOLLARS

← ### *GOOD*

There must be a slight rim for both obverse and reverse. LIBERTY on headband will be worn off. Date and all letters in legends must be plain and readable.

VERY GOOD →

At least any three letters of word LIBERTY on headband must show.

← ### *FINE*

Although weak, all seven letters of word LIB-ERTY in headband must show including letter "Y."

VERY FINE →

All seven letters of word LIBERTY on headband must be strong.

← ### *EXTREMELY FINE*

All seven letters of word LIBERTY on headband must be very bold. Top and bottom edges of ribbon on which LIBERTY is located must be well defined.

ABOUT UNCIRCULATED

Only a trace of wear will show on Liberty's head in front and cheek. Only slight wear will show on puff of Liberty's cap and on eagle's neck and wing tips.

HALF DOLLAR — Liberty Walking, 1916-1947

For the obverse, full length figure of Liberty is walking towards the rising sun, symbolizing the beginning of a new era. The folds of the stars and stripes blowing in the breeze form a background for her. Her right hand is outstretched in a gesture of peace; in her right arm, she cradles a bundle of oak and laurel leaves, symbolizing civil and military glory. The whole is surrounded by a wide-spaced LIBERTY. Rising sun has thirteen rays. IN GOD WE TRUST is in two lines to the right of the figure; date is below figure.

For the reverse, eagle — very realistic and fierce looking — stands on a lofty crag, facing left with upraised wings. To the right of the forward talon is a sapling of Mountain Pine growing in a crevice of the rock. E PLURIBUS UNUM is in two lines at the end of the branches of the sapling. UNITED STATES OF AMERICA is in circular arrangement at the top. Below eagle is the denomination, HALF DOLLAR. Except for 1916-17 when the mint mark was for some issues on the obverse, the mint mark is regularly found on the reverse underneath the sapling.

1916-1920

FAIR

Coin will be identified as to type and date.

ABOUT GOOD

Rim on reverse will be worn down into letters of legend.

HALF DOLLARS

GOOD

Slight rim for both obverse and reverse must show. Most of the motto, **IN GOD WE TRUST**, will be plain and readable.

←   *VERY GOOD*

Motto, **IN GOD WE TRUST**, must stand out. Although not bold, the word **GOD** must show all three letters. Traces of lines in Liberty's skirt must show.

FINE   →

About half the lines in Liberty's skirt in the deepest recesses must show. There will be no lines down the legs but about one-third of the lines in the sandal on Liberty's left foot must show.

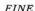

←   *VERY FINE*

Lines of Liberty's skirt will show but not be complete. Lines in sandal on left foot will be complete but not bold. There will be faint traces of lines down towards bottom of skirt on left leg. Breast and right arm will show some wear.

EXTREMELY FINE   →

There will be partial lines in skirt down right leg and a few lines in skirt — towards bottom — along left leg. There will be very little wear on right arm and breast.

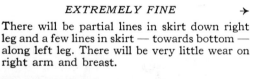

HALF DOLLARS
ABOUT UNCIRCULATED

There will be only a trace of wear on Liberty's head, right arm, right leg and foot. Only partial lines will show on left leg towards bottom of skirt. Slight wear will show on eagle's body between breast and left wing and on eagle's left leg.

Special Notation: Lines on Liberty's skirt for these years are very shallow and not too well defined. After 1916, the lines became better defined and deeper each succeeding year until 1921 when they became quite bold.

1921-1947
FAIR
Not collectable.

ABOUT GOOD
Rim will be worn down into letters on reverse.

GOOD
Obverse and reverse must show a slight rim. Most of the motto, IN GOD WE TRUST, will be readable and plain.

VERY GOOD
Motto, IN GOD WE TRUST — must stand out. The word, GOD, must show all three letters plainly. Approximately half of the lines of Liberty's skirt in front of left leg and the right leg must show plainly.

FINE
All lines in Liberty's skirt must show although the lines down left leg and the right leg will be worn considerably in spots. All of the lines in sandal on Liberty's left foot must show.

VERY FINE
All lines in skirt must be sharp including those down left and right legs. There will be very little wear on breast and right arm.

EXTREMELY FINE
All lines in skirt will be very bold, including those down left and right legs.

ABOUT UNCIRCULATED
There will be a trace of wear only on all high spots: right arm, head, left leg. On reverse, only slight wear will show on eagle's breast and left leg.

HALF DOLLAR — Franklin, 1948-1963

For the obverse, a large portrait of Benjamin Franklin faces right. LIBERTY in large letters is at top over head. Date is to the right of the neck. IN GOD WE TRUST is in large letters at the bottom, immediately under the bust.

For the reverse, the main device is portrait of Liberty Bell hanging. E PLURIBUS UNUM in very small letters is to left of bell; a stylized small eagle stands to right of bell. UNITED STATES OF AMERICA is at top; denomination is at bottom. Mint marks are immediately beneath letter "E" in word, STATES, on reverse.

FAIR, ABOUT GOOD and GOOD

Not collectable.

VERY GOOD

Coin will have a good rim for both obverse and reverse. Crack in Liberty Bell on reverse will show but be badly worn. Initials, JRS, on obverse under the bust will be worn but readable.

FINE

Initials, JRS, under the bust will be more distinct and clearly separated.

HALF DOLLARS

VERY FINE

At least half of the lower and upper incused lines on the rim of the Liberty Bell must show.

EXTREMELY FINE

At least two-thirds of the lower and upper incused lines on the rim of the Liberty Bell must show.

ABOUT UNCIRCULATED

All of the lower and upper incused lines on the rim of the Liberty Bell must show but they will be worn in one or two very small spots.

HALF DOLLARS
HALF DOLLAR — John F. Kennedy, 1964 to Date

The John F. Kennedy half dollar was authorized by Act of Congress and approved by President Lyndon Johnson on December 30, 1963.

The obverse of the coin carries a portrait of President Kennedy facing left; at the top and around in large letters is **LIBERTY**. Underneath the portrait at the bottom is the date. The motto **IN GOD WE TRUST** is at the left and right of the neck. The obverse was designed by Gilroy Roberts, chief engraver of the Philadelphia mint.

The reverse of the Kennedy half dollar carries a replica of the presidential coat-of-arms. At the top and around is the legend, **UNITED STATES OF AMERICA**; at the bottom in large letters is the value, **HALF DOLLAR**. The motto **E PLURIBUS UNUM** is on the ribbon just above the eagle's head. The reverse is the design of Frank Gasparro, assistant chief engraver of the Philadelphia mint.

At this time only two grades will be considered for the Kennedy half dollar: Extremely Fine and About Uncirculated.

EXTREMELY FINE

For the obverse there will be a small amount of wear on the hair above the ear and in line with the top of the forehead as well as on the jawbone, cheek and the top of the ear. For the reverse, there will be definite wear on the wings from the tip to the first joint as well as on the head of the eagle.

ABOUT UNCIRCULATED

For the obverse there will be a trace of wear on the hair above the ear and in line with the top of the forehead and on the jawbone. For the reverse, there will be a slight amount of wear on eagle's wings only around the first joint from tip of wings.

SILVER DOLLARS
DOLLAR — Flowing Hair, Small Eagle, 1794-1795

For the obverse, Liberty with flowing hair is the main device. **LIBERTY** is at the top in circular arrangement. On the left of **LIBERTY** are eight six-pointed stars; on the right, seven stars. Date is underneath the bust.

For the reverse, unrealistic small eagle is poised for flight and standing on a rock. Around eagle is a wreath of laurel tied at the bottom with a ribbon. In circular arrangement on outer field of coin is legend, **UNITED STATES OF AMERICA**. On edge of coin is notation: **ONE HUNDRED CENTS . . . ONE DOLLAR . . . OR UNIT.**

FAIR

Coin will be identified as to type and date.

ABOUT GOOD

Rim on reverse will be worn down into top of letters of legend.

SILVER DOLLARS

GOOD

Bust on obverse and eagle on reverse will be well outlined but show no details. All lettering and the date will be readable.

VERY GOOD

Major facial details for Liberty will show. All lettering on reverse will be plain but worn.

FINE

Ends of hair strands of Liberty will be visible with some detail. Top of hair above forehead will be outlined but worn smooth. All other hair details will be worn smooth.

SILVER DOLLARS

VERY FINE

Top of Liberty's hair above forehead will be worn slightly. Hair on side of head will show some details.

EXTREMELY FINE

Hair below head and down neck of Liberty will be defined and detailed but will show some wear.

ABOUT UNCIRCULATED

Hair roll above forehead of Liberty will show only slight wear. Facial features will be very plain and hair will be well outlined and detailed. Only slight wear will show on Liberty's eyebrow.

DOLLAR — Draped Bust, Small Eagle, 1795-1798

For the obverse, there is a draped bust of Liberty whose flowing hair is caught up by a fillet or ribbon; the bow ends of ribbon are prominent. The number of stars to the right and left of **LIBERTY** at the top varies. Date is underneath the bust and also varies in size.

For the reverse, the design is somewhat similar to that of the 1794-1795 issue except that the wreath is made up of laurel on the left and palm on the right; the ends of the wreath are tied together with ribbon. The whole is encircled with legend, **UNITED STATES OF AMERICA.** On the edge of the coin is notation: **ONE HUNDRED CENTS . . . ONE DOLLAR . . . OR UNIT.**

FAIR

Coin will be identified as to type and date.

ABOUT GOOD

Rim will be worn into top of legend on reverse. Date, stars and **LIBERTY** on obverse must show.

SILVER DOLLARS

GOOD

Liberty's bust on obverse and eagle on reverse will be outlined but show no detail. Some leaves of the wreath will show only faintly. Date must be readable.

VERY GOOD

Only the deepest folds at the bottom of Liberty's draped bust will show. All other drapery lines will be worn smooth. Hair from forehead down past ear and neck will be worn smooth. Curls at end of hair will be outlined.

FINE

All drapery lines on Liberty's bust will show but not be sharp. Hair from forehead, down past ear and neck will be outlined but show only slight detail.

SILVER DOLLARS

VERY FINE

Drapery lines from a point just left of breast cleavage to point halfway around to left will show only slight wear. From there to hair curls, the drapery will be worn about smooth.

EXTREMELY FINE

All lines in drapery on Liberty's bust will show distinctly around to hair curls. Hair will be well outlined and detailed.

ABOUT UNCIRCULATED

Only a trace of wear will show on the highest points of obverse and reverse: hair at top of forehead and immediately back of eye and Liberty's eyebrow; breast and left leg of eagle.

DOLLAR — Draped Bust, Heraldic Eagle, 1798-1804

For the obverse, the design is the same as for the 1795-1798 type dollar.

For the reverse, there is a large heraldic eagle across whose neck is a ribbon scroll bearing the motto E PLURIBUS UNUM. Right talon of eagle grasps a bundle of arrows; the left, an olive branch. Immediately above eagle is a galaxy of stars underneath an array of clouds. The whole is encircled by the legend, UNITED STATES OF AMERICA. On edge is notation: ONE HUNDRED CENTS . . . ONE DOLLAR . . . OR UNIT.

FAIR

Coin will be identified as to date and type.

ABOUT GOOD

Rim on reverse will be worn down into top of letters. Date, Stars and LIBERTY on obverse must show.

SILVER DOLLARS

GOOD

All of motto, **E PLURIBUS UNUM**, will be worn away. Lettering and date must be plain.

VERY GOOD

There will be only a partial showing of letters in **E PLURIBUS UNUM**. Only the deepest folds at the bottom of Liberty's draped bust will show. All other drapery lines will be worn smooth. Hairlines from forehead down past ear and neck will be worn smooth.

FINE

All drapery lines on Liberty's bust will show but will not be sharp. Hair from forehead, past ear and down neck will be well outlined but show only slight detail.

SILVER DOLLARS

VERY FINE

Drapery lines from point just left of breast cleavage to point halfway around to left will show only slight wear. From there to hair curls, the drapery will be worn about smooth.

EXTREMELY FINE

All lines in drapery on Liberty's bust will show distinctly around to hair curls. Hair will be outlined and detailed.

ABOUT UNCIRCULATED

There will be only a faint trace of wear on the very highest points: hair above forehead, drapery on bust and shoulders.

DOLLAR — Liberty Seated, 1840-1873

1840-1865

For the obverse, classic figure of Liberty, seated on a rock and wearing a Greek chiton, holds in left hand a pole atop of which is a Liberty Cap. Her right hand holds in place a shield. Across shield is a scroll on which is inscribed **LIBERTY**. In circular arrangement around top and sides are thirteen stars. Date is below seated figure.

For the reverse, the main device is an eagle defiant on whose breast is a shield. Eagle's right talon grasps an olive branch; the left, three arrows. The whole is surrounded by the legend **UNITED STATES OF AMERICA**. Underneath eagle at bottom is value: **ONE DOL**. Mint marks are between eagle and denomination on reverse.

1866-1873

For the obverse, the design is the same as for 1840-1865. The design for the reverse is the same except there is a scroll above head of eagle; on scroll is inscribed motto, **IN GOD WE TRUST**.

Note: Grading is the same for both types.

SILVER DOLLARS

FAIR

Coin will be identified as to date and type.

ABOUT GOOD

Rim will be worn down into letters on reverse.

GOOD

LIBERTY on shield on obverse will not show. All letters in legends and the date must show. There must be a distinct rim for both obverse and reverse.

SILVER DOLLARS

VERY GOOD

Any three letters of LIBERTY should be at least two-thirds complete.

FINE

All seven letters of word LIBERTY on shield must show even though they may be worn and appear weak.

VERY FINE

All seven letters of word LIBERTY on shield must show and be strong. Scroll on which LIBERTY is located will show some wear.

SILVER DOLLARS

EXTREMELY FINE

LIBERTY on shield will be very bold.
All horizontal lines at top of shield must
be complete. Edges of scroll on which
LIBERTY is located will be well defined. Clasp on left shoulder must be
plain. Head, skirt and cap will show
wear. On reverse, eagle's eye must be
plain with lines at top of shield on eagle's
breast complete.

ABOUT UNCIRCULATED

Only slight wear will show on Liberty's
breast, hair and legs from thigh to knee
cap. Only a trace of wear will show on
eagle's neck, wing tips and top of shield
on reverse.

DOLLAR — Morgan, 1878-1904; 1921

For the obverse, classic head of Liberty faces left. She wears a Liberty Cap on the front of which is inscribed **LIBERTY**. An array of agricultural products, including two heads of wheat and two cotton blossoms with leaves of each, adorns the front of cap just back of **LIBERTY** and down the side. Her hair falls in loose curls to bottom of truncated neck, revealing lower half of ear. Date is immediately underneath the neck. **E PLURIBUS UNUM** is in circular arrangement at top with seven stars on one side and six on the other.

For the reverse, eagle with outstretched wings holds olive branch in right talon and three arrows in left. First year of issue saw eagle with eight tail feathers; subsequent years, seven tail feathers. **IN GOD WE TRUST** is straight line above eagle. Laurel wreath, tied at bottom with ribbon bow, encircles lower part of eagle upward to wings. **UNITED STATES OF AMERICA** is broken by wings of eagle. **ONE DOLLAR** in circular arrangement at bottom. Mint marks are below knot of ribbon of wreath.

FAIR

Not collectable.

ABOUT GOOD

Not collectable.

SILVER DOLLARS

GOOD

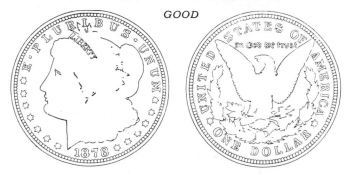

There will be a complete LIBERTY on headband. Rest of coin on both obverse and reverse will be worn considerably but all lettering and date will be plain.

VERY GOOD

Hair above forehead on Liberty's head will show considerable wear. Rest of hair details will be worn. Eagle's breast will be worn smooth; about half of eagle's wing tips will be worn smooth.

FINE

About half of the hairlines from top of head to ear must show. Hair above forehead will be outlined but worn. Ear must show distinctly.

SILVER DOLLARS

VERY FINE

About two-thirds of hairlines from top of forehead to ear must show very plainly. Ear must be well defined. Hair above forehead will be very plain. Feathers on eagle's breast will show plainly except at the very center.

EXTREMELY FINE

All hairlines will be very plain though showing some wear. Ear must be bold with lines raised. Wing tips of eagle and eagle's breast will show some wear but all details will be very plain.

ABOUT UNCIRCULATED

Only a trace of wear will show on hair above eye and above forehead of Liberty. On reverse, only a trace of wear will show on eagle's breast and wing tips.

Special Notation: Most silver dollars will have slight bag marks as a rule. Pronounced bag marks on uncirculated specimens will lower the grade.

DOLLAR — Peace, 1921-1935

For the obverse, the main device is a young head of Liberty. On her brow is a coronet of alternating long and short spikes. Across the front part of her head is a loose braid which continues on around her head and falls with other hair in wind-blown fashion. Hair at back of head is loosely knotted. Truncated neck separates motto, **IN GOD WE TRVST.** Date is below head. **LIBERTY** in widely spaced letters is at the top.

For the reverse, life-like eagle with head alert and wings folded faces symbolic rays of sun at lower right of coin. The eagle stands on a rocky crag across which is a spray of olive. Denomination, in a straight line, is broken by eagle's body. **UNITED STATES OF AMERICA** and **E PLURIBUS UNUM** are in two circular lines at top of coin. Mint marks are close to tip of eagle's wings. **PEACE** is at bottom of crag on which eagle is perched.

FAIR

Not collectable.

ABOUT GOOD

Not collectable.

SILVER DOLLARS

GOOD

All lettering and date must be readable although the word **PEACE** on reverse will be practically worn away.

VERY GOOD

The word **PEACE** on reverse must be complete although some letters will be faint.

FINE

The word **PEACE** on reverse will be plain. **E PLURIBUS UNUM** will be weak but readable. Right wing of eagle will be outlined but only a few feathers will show.

SILVER DOLLARS
VERY FINE

Hair above Liberty's eye will be outlined but will be worn considerably. Hair above ear will show wear but individual strands will be well defined. A few feathers on top and outside edge of right wing will show on the eagle.

EXTREMELY FINE

All hairlines above the eye and ear of Liberty will be slightly flattened by wear but still very bold. All feathers on top and outside edge of eagle's right wing will show but not too distinctly.

ABOUT UNCIRCU- LATED

Only a small amount of wear will show on hair above eye and ear of Liberty. Slight wear on top and outside edge of eagle's right wing.

Special Notation: On uncirculated specimens, pronounced bag marks will always lower the grade.

SILVER DOLLARS

TRADE DOLLARS

DOLLAR — Trade, 1873-1885

For the obverse, there is a seated figure of Liberty. She is clothed in classic chiton and is barefooted. She sits enthroned on a bale of cotton with a shock of grain at her back. The shock of grain rests on a grassy plot. To the right of Liberty's legs and feet is a large log. On her head is a coronet with hair knotted and falling in loose curls over her shoulder. Her right hand is extended and holds a sprig of olive; her left hand at her side holds a scarf on which is lettered the word, LIBERTY. At the base of the figure is a scroll on which is lettered the words IN GOD WE TRUST. Around outer edge are stars.

For the reverse, a bold, defiant eagle is the main device. He holds in right talon a cluster of three arrows and in the left talon, a laurel branch. Immediately under eagle is weight and fineness. Over the eagle is a scroll on which is inscribed E PLURIBUS UNUM. UNITED STATES OF AMERICA is around design at top and TRADE DOLLAR at bottom. Mint marks are above letter "D" in DOLLAR.

FAIR

Not collectable.

ABOUT GOOD

Rim will be worn down into letters on reverse and stars on obverse.

TRADE DOLLARS

GOOD

IN GOD WE TRUST on obverse will be worn off but there must be a slight rim. On reverse, E PLURIBUS UNUM will be gone but again there must be a slight rim. All other letters in legends and the date should be plain.

VERY GOOD

IN GOD WE TRUST should be partially visible. About one-half of E PLURIBUS UNUM must be visible. Definite rim should show for both obverse and reverse.

FINE

All of E PLURIBUS UNUM must be present although the lettering will be worn. All of IN GOD WE TRUST must be present although worn. All of word LIBERTY must show although worn.

TRADE DOLLARS

VERY FINE

E PLURIBUS UNUM, IN GOD WE TRUST and LIBERTY must
show and be strong, but show definite wear.

EXTREMELY FINE

E PLURIBUS UNUM, IN GOD WE
TRUST and LIBERTY must be very
sharp. There will be very little wear on
rims — obverse and reverse.

ABOUT UNCIRCULATED

Only traces of wear will show on wheat
shock, head, shoulder and knee cap of Liberty. There will be slight wear on eagle's
head and left wing. All legends and mottoes
must be very bold.

Special Notation: Uncirculated coins will show no wear except on Liberty's head and hand, caused by stacking new coins. Pronounced bag
marks on uncirculated specimens will lower the grade. Chop marks will not
lower the grade as long as they are not in vital places or too numerous.

GOLD DOLLARS — Type I, 1849-1854

For the obverse, classic head of Liberty faces left. There is a coronet on her head. On the coronet is inscribed LIBERTY. The coronet has rounded prongs on top. Hair is combed straight back from coronet into hair knot. Loose hair puffs encircle head beneath coronet and several curls hang down her neck. Thirteen six-pointed stars completely encircle the head.

For the reverse, large "1" is near top; DOLLAR is immediately underneath. The date is below the word, DOLLAR. An open wreath of laurel encircles the denomination and date. UNITED STATES OF AMERICA is in circular arrangement at top. Mint marks are underneath wreath on reverse.

FAIR

Collectable only as a charm.

ABOUT GOOD

Collectable only as a space filler.

GOOD

LIBERTY on headband will be worn away. All letters and the date must be plain.

VERY GOOD
Partial LIBERTY on headband will show.

GOLD DOLLARS

FINE

There will be a full **LIBERTY** on the headband. However, all main hairlines will be worn smooth as well as the knobs at the top of the coronet.

VERY FINE

There will be a full **LIBERTY** on the headband. The knobs at the top of the coronet will be outlined partially.

EXTREMELY FINE

There will be very little wear on Liberty's hair and the knobs at the top of the coronet must stand out.

ABOUT UNCIRCULATED

Only a trace of wear will show on Liberty's hairlines below the coronet.

Special Notation: On all Gold Dollars — especially Type III, the word **LIBERTY** is not well struck. This may be seen on even uncirculated specimens.

GOLD DOLLARS — Type II, 1854-1856

Type II Gold Dollars are larger in diameter than Type I and thinner.

For the obverse, large head of Liberty faces left with a feathered head-dress or crown atop her head. Feathers are closely set in a beaded head-band on which is inscribed LIBERTY. Feathers are curled at top with curl facing out. Heavy hair curls fall to the shoulder of Liberty. The whole is encircled by the legend, UNITED STATES OF AMERICA.

For the reverse, numeral "1," DOLLAR and date are in three straight lines. The whole is encircled by a wreath of corn, cotton, wheat and tobacco. Mint marks are underneath wreath on reverse.

FAIR

Collectable only as a charm.

ABOUT GOOD

Collectable only as a space filler.

GOOD

Feathers on headdress, hair down Liberty's neck and the word LIBERTY on the headband will be partially worn away.

VERY GOOD

Outline of the tips of feathers and the feathers them-selves in Liberty's headdress will be worn consider-ably but be identifiable.

GOLD DOLLARS

FINE

Tips of feather curls on headdress will be partially worn away.

VERY FINE

Tips of feather curls on headdress will be well outlined but show no details.

EXTREMELY FINE

There will be a slight amount of wear on tips of feather curls on headdress.

ABOUT UNCIRCULATED

There will be only a faint trace of wear on feather curls and the hair below the headdress.

Special Notation: The majority of these coins were struck in such a way as to be bent. They can be straightened out easily without impairing the coin. Place the bent coin between two pieces of soft pine. Strike with hammer directly over the coin. Don't overdo. Many 1855-D Gold Dollars have a poor date.

GOLD DOLLAR — Type III, 1856-1889

For the obverse, the design is generally the same as for the 1854-1856 Gold Dollar except the head of Liberty is larger. For the reverse, the design is the same as for the 1854-1856 Gold Dollar. Mint marks are found underneath the wreath on the reverse.

FAIR

Collectable only as a charm.

ABOUT GOOD

Collectable only as a space filler.

GOOD

The word LIBERTY on headband will be worn away. All lettering and the date must be plain.

VERY GOOD

At least any three letters in word LIBERTY on headband must be visible. Date and lettering must be plain.

GOLD DOLLARS

FINE

There will be a full LIBERTY on the headband but the beads above the headband will be worn partially. Curled feathers at the top of the headband will be worn flat and will show no detail.

VERY FINE

Liberty's eyebrow will be worn. Hair under the headdress from forehead to about two-thirds of the distance back will be worn. Hair to the right of the ear will be worn as well as the bottom curl on neck. Curled feathers at top of headdress will show slight detail.

EXTREMELY FINE

There will be a trace of wear above and to the right of Liberty's eye. There will be only slight amount of wear on top of curled feathers of headdress.

ABOUT UNCIRCULATED

Only a very faint trace of wear will be visible on top of the curled feathers and hair above Liberty's eye.

Special Notation: Gold Dollars of this issue were not always struck well at the mint. Coins of this nature can be graded satisfactorily only by an expert.

QUARTER EAGLE — Bust, 1796-1807

For the obverse, round-faced Liberty, changing slightly in appearance almost every year of this type and wearing peaked cap, faces right. Her hair generally puffs over her forehead and falls in strands to her shoulder. For some years, there is a wind-blown appearance to parts of her hair. For the 1796 issue, LIBERTY appears with and without stars on either side. LIBERTY varies in position from that immediately over head to that slightly right of head. Date is underneath bust.

For the reverse, large heraldic eagle with shield on breast is the main device. Galaxy of thirteen stars are immediately above head of eagle. Above stars is a circular arrangement of clouds. Across neck of eagle is a ribbon on which is inscribed E PLURIBUS UNUM. Eagle carries bundle of arrows in right talon and an olive branch in the left talon. Whole is partially surrounded by UNITED STATES OF AMERICA.

FAIR

Collectable only as a charm.

ABOUT GOOD

Collectable only as a space filler.

GOOD

On reverse, the motto on scroll will be completely worn away. All other lettering and the date will be plain.

QUARTER EAGLES

VERY GOOD

Liberty's hair will be well outlined but all details will be worn smooth. There will be only a partial motto, **E PLURIBUS UNUM**, on the reverse.

FINE

Liberty's hair will be outlined but the highest parts will be worn. **E PLURIBUS UNUM** on reverse will be readable but not bold.

VERY FINE

There will be definite wear on all high points of Liberty's hair and turban. On the reverse, highest points of the eagle's wing tips, head and the scroll with clouds above will show slight wear.

EXTREMELY FINE

There will be a slight amount of wear on Liberty's hair and the highest part of her cheek.

ABOUT UNCIRCULATED

There will be traces of wear on Liberty's cap, hair and folds of the drapery on her bust.

Special Notation: The motto, E PLURIBUS UNUM, will not always be complete even on uncirculated specimens.

QUARTER EAGLE — Bust Facing Left, Round Cap, 1808-1834

For the obverse, a matronly looking bust of Liberty with round cap faces left. Curls project out from under cap over forehead and at back, falling to shoulders. LIBERTY is lettered on band across front of cap. 1808 issue has stars on outer edge, seven on one side and six on other side of bust. For balance of this type, the stars — wide-spaced — encircle the head. Date is underneath the bust.

For the reverse, smaller eagle with shield on breast is main device. Olive branch is held by right talon; arrows, by left. Ribbon above eagle carries motto, E PLURIBUS UNUM. Whole is partially surrounded by legend, UNITED STATES OF AMERICA. Denomination, 2½ D., is at the bottom.

FAIR

Collectable only as a charm.

ABOUT GOOD

Collectable only as a space filler.

GOOD

On reverse, the motto, E PLURIBUS UNUM, will be worn away. All other lettering and the date must be plain.

VERY GOOD

At least half of the letters of E PLURIBUS UNUM must show on the reverse. There will be a partial LIBERTY on the headband on the obverse.

QUARTER EAGLES

FINE

Although weak, **E PLURIBUS UNUM** must be readable on reverse. All of **LIBERTY** on headband on obverse must be readable.

VERY FINE

E PLURIBUS UNUM and **LIBERTY** must be very plain.

EXTREMELY FINE

All details of Liberty's hair must be plain although showing slight wear.

ABOUT UNCIRCULATED

Only a trace of wear will show on Liberty's cap, highest portions of her hair and the folds of her gown.

QUARTER EAGLE — Fillet Type, 1834-1839

For the obverse, a more classic bust of Liberty faces left. Her hair is bound in front with a fillet or ribbon on which is lettered **LIBERTY**. Her hair falls in curls to the back. Thirteen stars encircle head and date is underneath head. Mint marks for 1838 and 1839 issues are over date.

For the reverse, the design is the same as for preceding type except the motto, **E PLURIBUS UNUM**, has been omitted.

QUARTER EAGLE — Coronet Type, 1840-1907

For the obverse, the head of Liberty is smaller and a coronet replaces the ribbon on which the word, **LIBERTY**, is lettered. For the reverse, the design is the same as for the Fillet Type. Mint marks are under eagle on reverse until 1879.

Note: Grading is the same for both types.

FAIR

Collectable only as a charm.

ABOUT GOOD

Collectable only as a space filler.

GOOD

LIBERTY on headband will be worn away but all other lettering and the date will be readable.

QUARTER EAGLES

VERY GOOD

There will be a partial **LIBERTY** on the headband. Hair curl directly below Liberty's ear will be barely outlined.

FINE

Hair curl directly below Liberty's ear will be outlined very plainly but with no detail. **LIBERTY** will be complete and readable.

VERY FINE

Hair curl below Liberty's ear will be outlined with all details present but will show wear. **LIBERTY** on headband must stand out plainly.

EXTREMELY FINE

There will be slight wear on top of Liberty's head and the hair which is just below the "L" in **LIBERTY**. For the coronet type, the top of Liberty's coronet will show some wear. On the reverse, the upper part of eagle's wings and the neck will show a small amount of wear.

ABOUT UNCIRCULATED

There will be a trace of wear on top of Liberty's head and top of the front part of the coronet.
Special Notation: Be very cautious about buying 1848 quarter eagles with "CAL" above eagle on reverse. Specimens should be purchased from reputable dealers as this type is easily faked and hard to detect.

QUARTER EAGLE — Indian Head, 1908-1929

For the obverse, the main device is an incused head of Indian in full war bonnet. LIBERTY at top of coin and stars on either side are all incused. Incused date is underneath the head.

For the reverse, all designs and lettering are incused. Majestic eagle, facing left with right leg thrust forward, stands on closely bound bundle of arrows. An olive branch is in front of arrow bundle, extending beyond arrowheads to left. Eagle's right talon holds branch against the bundle. E PLURIBUS UNUM to the left of the eagle. UNITED STATES OF AMERICA is at top in circular arrangement. Denomination is underneath eagle. Mint marks are to the left of bundle of arrows.

FAIR

Collectable only as a charm.

ABOUT GOOD

Collectable only as a space filler.

GOOD

Date must be plain. The cord and band on the Indian's war bonnet will be worn smooth. All lettering must be readable.

VERY GOOD

Outline of cord on Indian's war bonnet must show and not be smooth as well as feathers on top of head.

FINE

The knot in hair cord must show but small feathers on top of head will be faint.

VERY FINE

Knot in hair cord must be very distinct. Small feathers on top of head will be plain. Indian's cheekbone will be worn down about halfway.

EXTREMELY FINE

A spot of wear on the Indian's cheekbone will show. War bonnet must be very distinct with some wear. Decorative row of feathers on headband will show only slight wear.

ABOUT UNCIRCULATED

The zig-zag decorative line on the headband must be complete. Only slight wear will show on Indian's cheekbone.

Special Notation: On FINE or better specimens, the mint mark must be identified without any question. Coins of this type with bold mint marks command a better price than those with weak mint marks.

THREE DOLLAR GOLD — 1854-1889

For the obverse, large head of Liberty faces left with feathered headdress or crown atop her head. Feathers are set closely in a beaded headband on which is inscribed **LIBERTY**. Feathers are curled at the top with curl facing out. Heavy hair curls fall to the shoulder of Liberty. The whole is encircled by **UNITED STATES OF AMERICA**.

For the reverse, numeral "3," DOLLAR and date are in three straight lines, the whole encircled by an open wreath of cotton, corn, wheat and tobacco. For the 1854 Three Dollar Gold, the word DOLLAR is in smaller letters than for succeeding years. Mint marks will be under bow of wreath at bottom of coin.

FAIR

Collectable only as a charm.

◄   **ABOUT GOOD**

The word **LIBERTY** will be worn away. Lettering and date will be faint.

GOOD   →

The word **LIBERTY** on headband will be worn away. All lettering and date must be plain.

◄   **VERY GOOD**

At least any three letters of word **LIBERTY** on headband must be visible. Date and lettering must be plain.

THREE DOLLARS

FINE

Curled feathers at top of headdress will be worn
flat and show no details. There will be a full
LIBERTY on the headband but the beads
above the headband will be worn partially.

VERY FINE

Liberty's eyebrow will be worn. Hair under
headdress from forehead to about two-thirds'
distance back will be worn. Hair to the right
of the ear will be worn. Bottom curl on neck
will be worn. Curled feathers at top of headdress
will show only slight detail.

EXTREMELY FINE

There will be only a trace of wear above and
to the right of Liberty's eye. There will be a
slight amount of wear on top of curled feathers
of headdress.

ABOUT UNCIRCULATED

Only a faint trace of wear will be visible on top
of curled feathers and the hair above Liberty's
eye.

Special Notation: Uncirculated specimens must show no sign of wear.
The 1854-C and 1954-D issues will be poorly struck on reverse.

HALF EAGLE — Bust, 1795-1807

Small Eagle Type — 1795-1796

For the obverse, a round faced Liberty with peaked cap faces right. Hair puffs over forehead and falls in strands to shoulder. LIBERTY is at top right with ten six-pointed stars to the left and five stars to the right of LIBERTY. Date is below bust.

For the reverse, small unrealistic eagle with wings outstretched stands on an olive branch, holding a laurel wreath in its beak. UNITED STATES OF AMERICA around outer edge of coin.

Large Eagle Type — 1795; 1797-1807

For the obverse, there are the same general features as for the 1795-1796 issues with Liberty's hair in slightly different arrangements and appearance.

For the reverse, large heraldic eagle with shield on breast is main device. In eagle's right talon is bundle of arrows; in left, a sprig of olive. A galaxy of thirteen stars is above eagle's head; above head are clouds in circular arrangement. Eagle holds in his beak a scroll on which is inscribed **E PLURIBUS UNUM. UNITED STATES OF AMERICA** almost surrounds the eagle.

Note: Except as indicated, grading is same for both types.

FAIR
Collectable only as a charm.

ABOUT GOOD
Collectable only as a space filler.

HALF EAGLES

GOOD

Date and all lettering must be readable. On heraldic eagle reverse, there will be no **E PLURIBUS UNUM**.

VERY GOOD

Liberty's hair will be outlined but all details will be worn. On heraldic eagle reverse, **E PLURIBUS UNUM** will be readable but not bold.

FINE

Liberty's hair will be well outlined but the highest parts will be worn considerably. From 1797 on, **E PLURIBUS UNUM** on reverse will be readable but not bold.

[178]

HALF EAGLES

VERY FINE

There will be definite wear on all the highest points of Liberty's hair and turban but they will not be worn smooth. On reverse, highest points of eagle's wings and head will show slight wear.

EXTREMELY FINE

There will be slight wear on Liberty's hair and the highest part of cheek.

ABOUT UNCIRCULATED

There will be only a trace of wear on Liberty's hair, folds of her cap and drapery on bust.

Special Notation: These coins were all struck on the horse drawn press. Therefore, there will be a great variation of the motto and other features. In some cases, parts of a coin will be lightly struck; on others very bold. In case of any doubt, an expert should be consulted.

1807-1812

For the obverse of this type, matronly looking bust of Liberty with round cap on head faces left. Curls project out from edge of cap and fall to shoulder. LIBERTY is lettered on band across front of cap. From 1807-1812, thirteen stars are divided, seven on one side and six on other side of head. Date is underneath bust.

For the reverse, a small heraldic eagle grasps an olive branch in right talon and arrows in left talon. Circular scroll over head of eagle carries motto, **E PLURIBUS UNUM. UNITED STATES OF AMERICA** encloses the whole with denomination, 5 D, at bottom underneath the eagle.

Larger Head for Obverse — 1813-1834

For the obverse of this type, the head is larger with truncated neck. Thirteen stars are around head; date is underneath neck. For the reverse, the design is essentially the same as for the 1807-1812 type.

HALF EAGLES

1834-1838

For the obverse of this type there is no turban but a broad band restraining the hair. Liberty faces left. On the band there is the word LIBERTY. Thirteen stars are around the head; the date is underneath truncated neck.

For the reverse, the design is essentially the same as for preceding types except the scroll and E PLURIBUS UNUM have been removed.

Note: The same general method of grading is used for all three preceding types except as indicated.

FAIR

Collectable only as a charm.

ABOUT GOOD

Collectable only as a space filler.

GOOD

LIBERTY on headband and E PLURIBUS UNUM on reverse (from 1834-1838 there is no motto on reverse) will be worn away. All other lettering and date must be readable.

HALF EAGLES

There will be a partial **LIBERTY** on headband and a partial **E PLUR-IBUS UNUM** on reverse (from 1834-1838 there will be no motto).

FINE

There will be a full **LIBERTY** on the headband although weak in spots, especially towards the center.

VERY FINE

LIBERTY must stand out on headband although the top and bottom edges of the band will show slight wear. There will be definite wear on hair from a point just below word **LIBERTY** to the date.

HALF EAGLES

EXTREMELY FINE

There will be only slight wear on highest portions of Liberty's hair with approximately 80% of the major curls plain.

ABOUT UNCIRCULATED

There will be a trace of wear on the highest portions of hair and above word **LIBERTY** on the cap and high points of gown.

Special Notation: From 1807 through 1812, the clasp on Liberty's left shoulder must show the decorative motif plainly for about uncirculated specimens.

HALF EAGLE — Small Head with Coronet, 1839-1866

For the obverse, a more classic head of Liberty faces left. On her head is a coronet with **LIBERTY** on the front. Hair is pulled back in loose knot at back of head with curls falling down neck. Thirteen stars in circular arrangement at top; date is underneath truncated neck.

For the reverse, the design is essentially the same as for the previous issue except that now the denomination reads, **FIVE D.** Mint marks are under eagle.

FAIR

Collectable only as a charm.

ABOUT GOOD

Collectable only as a space filler.

GOOD

LIBERTY will be fairly well worn away with only a bare trace of the letters.

VERY GOOD

At least one-half of **LIBERTY** on headband must be readable.

HALF EAGLES

FINE

Liberty's hair down neck will be well outlined with no detail. All seven letters of LIBERTY will be readable.

VERY FINE

There will be a full LIBERTY on the headband with all letters plain. Hair down Liberty's neck will be worn but all major details will be visible.

EXTREMELY FINE

All details of Liberty's hair down neck will show. There will be slight wear on coronet at top. Lower part of coronet and hair will show slight wear.

ABOUT UNCIRCULATED

Only a trace of wear will show on top of coronet and highest portions of hair.

For the obverse, the design is the same as for the 1839-1866 issue. For the reverse, the design is the same as for the 1839-1866 issue except a graceful scroll has been added above the eagle's head carrying the motto, IN GOD WE TRUST. Mint marks are under eagle.

FAIR

Collectable only as a charm.

ABOUT GOOD

Collectable only as a space filler.

GOOD

IN GOD WE TRUST on reverse will be partially worn away. At least half of the motto must show and be readable.

VERY GOOD

IN GOD WE TRUST on reverse will be very weak in spots yet all of the motto will be present on coin.

HALF EAGLES

FINE

IN GOD WE TRUST on reverse will be worn but all letters will be plain and readable.

VERY FINE

There will be definite wear on obverse and reverse. About half of the hairlines will show above the coronet. Hair curls below the ear will be worn but plain. **IN GOD WE**

TRUST on reverse must be sharp, including the ribbon on which it is located.

EXTREMELY FINE

A trace of wear will show on top of Liberty's head and the hair which is just below the "L" of **LIBERTY**. Top part of crown will show some wear. On reverse, eagle's neck and upper part of wings will show small amount of wear.

ABOUT UNCIRCULATED

There will be a faint trace of wear on top of the coronet, hair on top of Liberty's head and just above her eye.

HALF EAGLE — Indian Head, 1908-1929

For the obverse and reverse, the design is the same as for the Quarter Eagle with Indian Head.

FAIR
Collectable only as a charm.

ABOUT GOOD
Collectable only as a space filler.

GOOD
Coin will be worn but all lettering and date will be readable.

VERY GOOD
Outline of cord on war bonnet will show and not be worn smooth as well as feathers on top of head.

FINE
The knot in the hair cord will show but the small feathers on top of head will be faint.

HALF EAGLES

VERY FINE

Cord on war bonnet will be worn considerably. Counting from the top, the third, fourth and fifth eagle feathers in war bonnet will also show considerable wear on highest

parts. Tip of eagle's wing on reverse will be worn about smooth and the feathers to about halfway down the wing will show considerable wear.

EXTREMELY FINE

Highest part of Indian's cheekbone will be worn away as well as the jawbone immediately underneath the cheekbone. Feathers on upper part of

the wing of eagle on reverse will be outlined but show considerable wear.

ABOUT UNCRICULATED

Cheekbone of Indian will show a faint trace of wear as well as the extreme upper part of wings of eagle on reverse.

Special Notation: The Indian Head Type of Half Eagle, dated 1909 with "O" mint mark, should not be purchased in any grade below VERY FINE. Fake "O's" are often made from 1909-D coins. On grades VERY FINE or better, the faked "O" can be easily recognized with a strong glass. Coins with bold mint marks will command a higher price.

Bust, Small Eagle — 1795-1797

For the obverse of this type, matronly bust of Liberty faces right. She wears a high turban. Her hair puffs out from under the turban in front and falls in heavy strands to her shoulder. One heavy strand is wound around the turbaned head. **LIBERTY** is at the upper right with five six-pointed stars to the right and ten stars to the left. Date is underneath the bust.

For the reverse, a small unrealistic eagle stands with wings outstretched on a palm branch. Eagle holds a laurel wreath in beak. **UNITED STATES OF AMERICA** on outer edge of coin.

Bust, Heraldic Eagle — 1797-1804

For the obverse, design is essentially the same as for the preceding issue except the number and arrangement of stars may differ.

For the reverse, large heraldic eagle is main device. Eagle holds in right talon a bundle of arrows and in the left, an olive branch. Across right wing and neck of eagle is a scroll on which is lettered **E PLURIBUS UNUM**. Galaxy of stars is immediately above head of eagle with clouds above stars. The whole is partially enclosed by **UNITED STATES OF AMERICA**.

EAGLES

FAIR
Collectable only as a charm.

ABOUT GOOD
Collectable only as a space filler.

GOOD
Although very much worn, all lettering and the date must be plain.

VERY GOOD
Head of Liberty and her turban must be outlined but there will be no details.

FINE
Head of Liberty and her turban will be outlined with most of the details present but worn.

VERY FINE
Most of the hair down Liberty's neck and around her turban and in front of her forehead will be well outlined without details.

EAGLES

EXTREMELY FINE

There will be definite wear on hair to the left of Liberty's eye and the strand of hair across and around her turban. Definite wear will show on eagle's wing tips.

ABOUT UNCIRCULATED

There will be traces of minor wear on Liberty's hair and the lines of her gown.

Special Notation: A GEM UNCIRCULATED specimen in this series will show practically no bag marks, scratches or wear. An UNCIRCULATED specimen will have very minor bag marks with no wear on turban or hair. On the reverse, there will be no signs of definite wear although on some issues, the left wing tip will be struck weak. In this series, due to the method of striking coins, defective dies, re-engraved dies, etc., there may be many minor defects. These will include flat hairlines, strengthened hairlines, weak stars on one side with bold stars on the other, etc. Actually, the verdict of an expert is needed to grade a coin of this series accurately.

EAGLE — Coronet, 1838-1866

For the obverse, a more classic and pleasing bust of Liberty faces left. On her head is a coronet on which is lettered **LIBERTY.** Her hair is knotted at the back and several curls fall down her neck to the shoulder. Thirteen six-pointed stars almost surround the bust on the outer edge of the coin. Date is underneath the bust.

For the reverse, a more natural looking eagle is main device with shield on breast. In right talon is the olive branch; in the left, three arrows. **UNITED STATES OF AMERICA** is in circular arrangement at the top. Denomination, **TEN D.**, is at bottom underneath eagle. Mint marks are underneath tail of eagle.

EAGLE — Coronet, 1866-1907

For the obverse, the design is the same as for preceding issue. For the reverse, the design is the same as for the preceding issue except a scroll has been added above the head of the eagle and carries the motto, **IN GOD WE TRUST.**

Note: Grading is the same for both types.

FAIR

Collectable only as a charm.

ABOUT GOOD

Collectable only as a space filler.

GOOD

LIBERTY will be almost worn away with only traces of letters present.

VERY GOOD

All of **LIBERTY** will show but will be very weak in spots.

FINE

LIBERTY must be completely readable with all letters present.

EAGLES

VERY FINE

About half of the hairlines will show above the coronet. Hair curls below the ear will be worn but plain.

EXTREMELY FINE

There will be a trace of wear on hair on top of Liberty's head and the hair which is just below the "L" in LIBERTY. Top part of the coronet will show some wear. On reverse, the upper part of wings and neck of eagle will show small amount of wear.

ABOUT UNCIRCULATED

There will be a faint trace of wear on top of the coronet, top of Liberty's hair and hair just above her eye.

Special Notation: GEM UNCIRCULATED eagles will show only minor bag and scuff marks.

EAGLES — Indian Head, 1907-1933

For the obverse, a girlish head of Liberty is main device. On her head is an Indian war bonnet. Loose strands of hair project from the bottom edge of the bonnet. Immediately above the war bonnet are thirteen six-pointed stars in close order. LIBERTY is in raised letters on band of the bonnet. Date is under head.

For the reverse, a bold defiant eagle stands on a compact bundle of arrows. Olive branch is in front of bundle and extends to the left. Branch is held against bundle by right talon of eagle. IN GOD WE TRUST (missing in the first year of issue) is to the left in front of eagle's breast. UNITED STATES OF AMERICA is at top in close order; TEN DOLLARS is at bottom underneath bundle of arrows. Mint marks are at left of bundle of arrows.

FAIR
Collectable only as a charm.

ABOUT GOOD
Collectable only as a space filler.

GOOD
The word LIBERTY on the headband will be worn smooth. On reverse, all lettering must be plain and readable.

VERY GOOD
Outer edges of feathers on headdress will be outlined with the center line of each feather smooth. Hair below headband will be worn and only a partial LIBERTY will show. On reverse, all

outline of feathers on eagle's left wing will be worn; all lines of arrows and heads of arrows will be worn.

EAGLES

FINE

On the obverse, a full **LIBERTY** is necessary but the feathers of the war bonnet will show definite wear. On the reverse, about half of the feather outlines of the eagle's left wing will be worn away. Leaves to the left of the eagle's perch will be worn and eagle's talons will be worn considerably.

VERY FINE

On obverse there will be some wear on feathers of Indian war bonnet where feathers join the headband. Highest points of hair below the headband will show some wear.

EXTREMELY FINE

There will be a slight amount of wear on Liberty's cheekbone and feathers of headdress. A slight amount of wear will show above eye of eagle and down eagle's left wing.

ABOUT UNCIRCULATED

There will be a trace of wear on Liberty's hair along her forehead and just above her eye. The front part of the eagle's wings on reverse will show a trace of wear.

Special Notation: **A GEM UNCIRCULATED** coin will show only very minor bag marks and no wear.

DOUBLE EAGLE — Liberty Head, 1849-1907

1850-1866

For the obverse of this issue, a well proportioned classic head of Liberty faces left. Hair is combed straight back to end in loose knot at back of head. Two loose curls fall down her neck. A coronet, on which is inscribed **LIBERTY**, is pressed firmly on front of head to make the hair puff. Thirteen six-pointed stars on outer edge of coin almost surround the head. Date is at bottom.

For the reverse, a stylized eagle is the main device. The eagle clutches an olive branch in right talon and three arrows in left talon. Above the eagle's head are thirteen six-pointed stars in oval arrangement. Immediately above the stars in circular arrangement with heavier and longer rays are sun rays, the whole giving a scalloped effect. On either side of eagle are ornate scrolls, the tips of which are superimposed on wings and tail of eagle. On left scroll, **E PLURIBUS**; on the right scroll, **UNUM**. **UNITED STATES OF AMERICA** is in circular arrangement at top; the denomination, **TWENTY D.**, is at the bottom. Mint marks are below tail of eagle.

1866-1907

For the obverse, the design is the same as for the preceding issue. For the reverse, the design is essentially the same except that the motto, **IN GOD WE TRUST**, in two lines has been included within the oval arrangement of stars above the eagle. From 1866 to 1876 the denomination, **TWENTY D.** is at the bottom; from 1877 to 1907, the denomination, **TWENTY DOLLARS**, is spelled out. Mint marks are below tail of eagle.

DOUBLE EAGLES

FAIR

Not collectable.

ABOUT GOOD

Collectable only as a charm.

GOOD

Collectable only as a space filler.

VERY GOOD

Last six rounded prongs of Liberty's crown will be worn away. There will be a partial LIBERTY and at least three letters must be distinct.

FINE

LIBERTY will be readable. Only the top half of the last seven rounded prongs of Liberty's crown will show. Other rounded prongs will be very plain. All hairlines will show considerable wear.

VERY FINE

All rounded prongs on Liberty's crown must be plain but the last seven or eight will show considerable wear. LIBERTY must be plain. There will be considerable wear on hair above Liberty's ear, in front of ear and to the right of ear.

DOUBLE EAGLES

EXTREMELY FINE

There will be a trace of wear on the rounded prongs of Liberty's crown and down the hair curls. There will be minor bag marks.

ABOUT UNCIRCULATED

Only a trace of wear will show on hair above eye and top of head; back portion of coronet above the ear.

Special Notation: Pronounced bag marks on uncirculated coins will lower the grade of the coins. **E PLURIBUS UNUM** on 1850 through 1876 variety will not always be completely readable on even **VERY FINE** specimens due to poor striking and abnormal wear on this particular spot.

DOUBLE EAGLE — Saint-Gaudens, 1907-1932

For the obverse, Liberty in classic garments stands on a rocky pinnacle. The left foot is planted firmly on a rock higher than surrounding terrain. Her hair and garments are wind-blown. Behind the full-length figure are stylized sun rays. In her right hand she holds a large torch, the flame bending in the wind. In her left hand, a large olive branch. Above her head is the word, **LIBERTY**. Date is to the right of Liberty's left ankle. For the 1907 issue, the date is in Roman numerals. From 1907 on, the date is in Arabic numerals. Forty-eight small stars almost encircle the whole design.

For the reverse, a large realistic eagle is in full flight to the left, reminiscent of the Gobrecht eagle. Beneath the eagle is the rising sun with stylized rays extending upward. **UNITED STATES OF AMERICA** is in circulated arrangement at top and immediately underneath the legend is denomination, **TWENTY DOLLARS**. From 1908 on, **IN GOD WE TRUST** is in raised letters on circular edge of sun. Mint marks are above date on obverse.

FAIR
Not collectable.

ABOUT GOOD
Collectable only as a charm.

GOOD
Collectable only as a space filler.

VERY GOOD
There will be definite wear down both legs and on chest of Liberty. Leaves below the date will be faint. Flame of torch and Liberty's fingers holding the torch will be worn away.

DOUBLE EAGLES

FINE

There will be considerable wear on Liberty's right leg from the crotch through foot. Garment on chest will be almost worn away. Liberty's nose will be worn almost flat. Leaves below date will be worn down. On reverse, tips of eagle's wings will be worn some.

VERY FINE

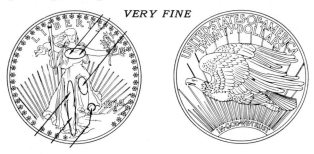

Contour of Liberty's breasts will be worn away. There will be minor wear on leaves below date and on right leg from crotch to and including toes. On reverse, top edge of left wing will show some feathers worn away. Side of eagle's breast will be worn to where feathers will not show.

EXTREMELY FINE

Lines of garment on chest must show with considerable wear on right breast. Definite wear will show on knee. On reverse, all feathers on breast and top edge of right wing of eagle must stand out.

DOUBLE EAGLES

ABOUT UNCIRCULATED

There will be a faint trace of wear on Liberty's right knee. A faint trace of wear will show on head and breast.

Special Notation: Uncirculated coins of this type will show a spot of wear on forehead, nose and right knee of Liberty which is caused by stacking the coins. All coins will show minor bag marks. Pronounced bag marks will lower the grade of uncirculated specimens.

APPENDIX

If You MUST Clean Your Coins

For some time now, a great debate has been going on among coin collectors: should a coin be cleaned? Older collectors contend stubbornly that under no circumstances should a coin ever be cleaned. On the other hand, there are those who take what is claimed to be a more sensible and practical viewpoint: there is a great demand today for Brilliant Uncirculated coins. To satisfy that demand means that for older coins as well as for recent issues, tarnish or oxidation must be removed safely without any harm to the finest coin.

In days gone by, better grades of coins were protected by wrapping in tissue paper or by keeping them in small white envelopes. All such paper contains a quantity of sulphur, causing both copper, silver and even nickel coins to darken. Coins exposed to strong sunlight over a period of time as well as coins stored in old purses, etc. will darken. In some cases, coins when turned in the light will reflect a variety of colors from their surface. Although somewhat darkened, these coins are considered by some collectors as quite desirable because they have "toned."

If you **MUST** clean your coins, consider only those which are **UNCIRCULATED** or **EXTREMELY FINE** with some mint luster. Use only a liquid cleaner which depends on chemical action for its cleaning power and not abrasion (similar to Vixen **SUPER DIP**). *Do not* use any kind of eraser no matter how soft; *do not* use any kind of paste polish, powders, baking soda, lemon juice, any kind of detergent or any liquid containing chlorine.

"Dipping" a silver or nickel coin is quite a distinct process. Actually, the coin should not be placed in the liquid cleaner. Rather a small cotton swab should be used, dipping the swab in the full-strength liquid cleaner and rubbing the surface of the coin in a circular motion. After the liquid cleaner has been rubbed on a number of times, don't let the coin stay out in the open air very long. Using Ivory soap, wash the coin thoroughly and rinse a number of times in running tepid water, rubbing lightly the surface of the coin with the wet ball of the thumb. Pat the coin dry with a soft cloth.

For copper and bronze coins, use the same technique as for silver and nickel coins except the liquid cleaner should be weakened by adding water (half and half). Repeat the process as many times as necessary but each time wash the coin with Ivory soap and rinse thoroughly. After final washing and rinsing, pat dry with a soft cloth.

This method, if followed correctly, will remove finger marks from **PROOF** coins without any trouble. It goes without saying that great care must be exercised in the handling of **PROOF** coins so that no damage will result. Be sure to hold the coin tightly between the index finger and thumb; be sure to apply the liquid cleaner with light circular motions of the cotton swab; be sure to wash and rinse thoroughly in tepid running water; be sure to pat — *not rub* — dry with a very soft cloth.

An **EXTREMELY FINE** or **UNCIRCULATED** silver or nickel coin on which a heavy black oxidation has formed a crust — especially between letters — can be cleaned effectively by soaking the coin for about 10 minutes in Worchestershire sauce. A soft tooth pick should be used to work in and around the letters and other spots where the black crust has formed. As a rule, all of the black encrustation will loosen and wash away as the coin is washed in Ivory soap and rinsed thoroughly. The coin may then be dipped in the manner previously described. *Please note:* neither this nor any other method of cleaning can help silver and nickel coins which have been burned.

For copper or bronze coins which have been buried in the earth over a long period of time or which have a heavy crust of oxidation, wrap the coin in several layers of gauze and place in pure olive oil. The olive oil should be in a glass jar and should cover the coin well. This process will take from three to eighteen months to show any material effect, depending on the condition of the coin. The gauze should be changed every now and then as well as the olive oil if it becomes too discolored. A coin cleaned in this manner will have a slightly oily sheen to it. *Do not* dip such a coin.

If you are not sure of the liquid cleaner at your disposal, by all means experiment with coins from your pocket before using on coins from your collection. Above all, *do not* use any liquid cleaner that is toxic.

Coins that have been dipped, washed, rinsed and dried should be allowed to return to room temperature before being stored. Be sure the coin is thoroughly dry.

Know Your Proofs

The old saying, "All that glitters is not gold," may be paraphrased "All that shines is not necessarily a proof coin."

Proof coins, especially the yearly sets, continue to be very popular with the beginning as well as the advanced collector. Lately, there has been considerable talk about Proof Sets being bought and sold in original containers and without even the brown Mint envelopes being opened.

The fact that a so-called Mint envelope shows no sign of being opened; the fact that apparently the plastic container has not been tampered with in any manner — all is not necessarily a guarantee that you, the buyer, are getting genuine Proof coins. Envelopes can be steamed open and now even the plastic container is being duplicated effectively. It's simply good business to open the brown envelope and examine all of the coins offered as Proofs with a strong glass. Thick plexiglass holders should be taken apart, if there is any doubt about the genuineness of a Proof set, so that coins may be examined closely with a strong glass.

The best insurance and assurance that the collector can have regarding Proof coins is to KNOW Proof coins. Too often the collector looks only at the highly polished surface of the coin which has been dubbed a Proof but nothing else.

For example unscrupulous individuals at times have substituted in 1936 Proof Sets Uncirculated coins which have been buffed to a high polish, using jeweler's rouge. More recently, 1960 Small Date Proof Sets have been sold with the 1960 Small Date Lincoln Cent not a Proof but a highly polished Uncirculated 1960 Small Date cent.

The collector who is not familiar with the appearance in depth of a Proof coin should take a little time to study these coins. Remember, Proof coins are struck on specially prepared planchets, struck with highly polished dies more slowly and with greater pressure than regular issue coins; that each coin is handled with gloved hands.

This is your cue then to observe the great clarity, sharpness and detail of all parts of the design of a coin — both obverse and reverse. Coins that are ordinarily struck very poorly for general circulation will show up very differently in Proof condition. No matter how highly polished the surface of a regular issue coin may be, it can't begin to compare with the surface of a Proof coin when examined closely with a strong glass.

Buy your Proof coins either from the Mint or from a reputable dealer; *do not* buy Proof coins from some "fly-by-night" individual who is here today and gone tomorrow.

So know your dealer and above all know your Proof coins when buying Proof coins or sets.